CONTENTS

THE HORSE

GENERAL MANAGEMENT

Julie Brega

J.A. Allen
London

British Library Cataloguing in Publication Data
A catalogue record for this book is available from the British Library

ISBN 0.85131.588.7

Published in Great Britain in 1993 by
J. A. Allen and Company Limited,
1 Lower Grosvenor Place,
Buckingham Palace Road,
London, SW1W 0EL.

(M)636.1 $

LIST OF
ILLUSTRATIONS

LIST OF TABLES

ACKNOWLEDGEMENTS

I would like to thank my friends Debby Baker and Kitty Best for all their help with this book: Debby for deciphering and typesetting the original manuscript and Kitty for the excellent diagrams.

Special thanks also to Bill, my husband, for his constant help and support.

INTRODUCTION

The Horse: General Management is one of six books in the Progressive Series. This series forms the basis of an advanced open learning course offered by The Open College of Equestrian Studies.

The main objective of these books is to present the information needed by the equestrian enthusiast in a clear and logical manner. This information is invaluable to everyone interested in horses, whether in a professional capacity as a yard manager or examination trainee, or as a private horse-owner.

The general management and nutrition of the horse, both stabled and at grass, are dealt with in this book. Stable construction and yard design, including aspects such as materials, ventilation and barn stabling, are clearly explained. The advantages and disadvantages of keeping a horse stabled are compared to those of keeping a horse at grass. The conclusion drawn is that a combined system, whereby the advantages of each may be enjoyed, should be employed, thus ensuring both the mental and physical well-being of the horse.

Under the heading 'The Horse at Grass', pasture management is covered. The quality of the pasture is dependent upon the way in which it is managed. Factors such as soil type, drainage, nutrient levels and weed eradication must be considered before deciding which fertilizers to use and grasses to sow. Other topics dealt with in this section include fencing, shelter, watering and feeding arrangements, haymaking, silage and haylage.

The major topic of feeding and nutrition is fully discussed, with examination of the nutrients and their importance in the diet, the digestive system and processes, feedstuffs, and the storage and release of energy. The method of calculating feed rations is clearly broken down into an easy to follow process; several sample feed charts are then presented. The dangers of internal parasites, their life cycles and control conclude the section on feeding and nutrition.

Instinctive equine behaviour is the final major heading, under which are covered topics such as the instincts of survival, sustenance, herd membership and defence, the ways in which horses communicate with each other as well as with humans, stable vices − their avoidance and control − and stress and its effects on the horse. Handling the fractious horse, methods of restraint, including twitching and sedation, and dealing with a cast horse are also dealt with.

The conclusion drawn is that the horse's mental wellbeing is as important as his physical wellbeing, and the horsemaster has 'got it right' when these two aspects are well balanced.

1

THE STABLED HORSE

The horse in his natural state roams freely, grazing at will, sleeping and breeding as nature dictates and always watchful for predators, but domestication has changed his lifestyle a great deal. In order to keep him fit and clean we now enforce long periods of confinement in a stable; time which need not be stressful to the horse, indeed some stables and levels of care and management verge on being luxurious.

The advantages of keeping a horse stabled are:

1) Convenience — stabling keeps the horse cleaner so reducing time to prepare him for exercise or for shows, etc.

2) It enables food and water intake to be monitored. Controlling the intake of grass helps to keep the horse fit.

3) It provides protection against cold and wet, heat, flies and midges.

4) It provides security, both from bullying by other horses and from thieves.

5) It saves grazing from becoming 'poached'.

The disadvantages of keeping a horse stabled are:

1) The horse's natural desires to wander and graze are denied.

1

2) The horse is unable to exercise himself.

3) Boredom may result.

4) It is labour intensive; constant attention is necessary.

The ideal situation is one whereby the horse is stabled during periods of bad weather and at night during the winter. In the summer he may be stabled during the day to protect him from the heat and flies and be turned out at night. Such a regime is known as the combined system.

Obviously a lot depends on the work programme of both horse and handler. The combined system can be adapted to suit the individual requirements of each horse, bearing in mind that sometimes summer weather is not much better than winter!

STABLE CONSTRUCTION

The site

The following points must be considered:

It must be level and well drained to provide a basis for dry, firm foundations. These must be wider than the base of the stable: if using sectional buildings, lay a concrete base upon which to erect them.

There should be access for vehicles.

Electricity and water supplies must be easily to hand.

It should preferably be near a house for security.

Is planning permission needed? Check with local authorities.

The soil

A subsoil of gravel or deep sand provides excellent drainage.

Limestone or chalk provide a firm base and fair drainage.

If building on clays, loams or marshy soils, great attention must be paid to subsoil drainage.

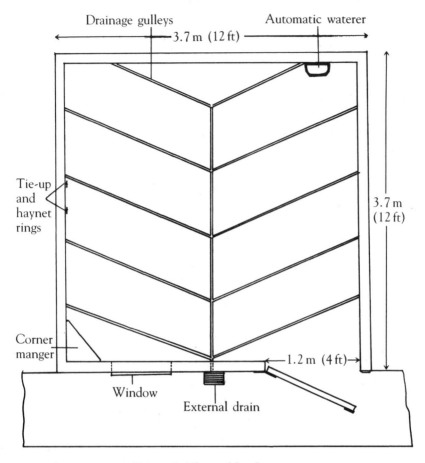

Figure 1 The stable plan

Well aerated soil provides good drainage. If the water table is high (subsoil water near the surface), then drainage is necessary.

Positioning

Good light and a free flow of air are essential.

When planning a yard, try to arrange the loose boxes in large squares. This enables the horses to see each other and watch the general yard duties, thus helping to prevent boredom. A square layout also helps with work efficiency: staff should not have to walk too far whilst carrying out their day-to-day chores.

Ideally stables should be sheltered from the cold north-easterly winds. This is another advantage of a square yard layout, protection is offered against the wind.

Dimensions

Loose boxes for ponies up to 14 hh   3.7 m × 3 m (12 ft × 10 ft)

Loose boxes for horses up to 16 hh   3.7 m × 3.7 m (12 ft × 12 ft)

Loose boxes for horses over 16 hh   3.7 m × 4.3 m (12 ft × 14 ft)

Materials

When choosing materials, safety should always be your chief consideration. Stables must be solidly built, draught-free and dry.

Good stabling is an investment. Most of the sectional buildings advertised in the equestrian magazines are built to very high standards and will last for many years. The main advantage of these buildings is that if you decide to move house you can take the stables with you.

Bricks make good solid stables but can prove expensive. Before erecting any form of stabling it is wise to contact the local authority to discuss the building regulations.

Walls should be at least 3.7 m (12 ft) high. If sloping, the lowest point must be at least 3 m (10 ft) high. The damp-proof course must be built into all brick walls a little above ground level.

Kicking boards up to 1.2 m (4 ft) high should be used on all wooden walls for extra strength and security.

The roof

1) Sloping roofs are best because rainwater will run down to the guttering rather than sitting on the roof. Ensure that adequate guttering and downpipes are used. The downpipes should lead to a drain as opposed to a water butt which may overflow.

2) The roof should be durable, noiseless, non-flammable and maintain an even temperature in all weathers. (Insulation in the roof will help maintain an even temperature.)

3) Suitable roofing materials include tiles and slates which, although they may break, come loose and leak, are excellent with regular maintenance. Roofing felt is a very popular and relatively cheap form of waterproofing a wooden roof. Corrugated heavy duty plastic also fulfils the requirements.

   Materials not suitable for roofing are thatch — because of the maintenance, vermin and fire risk — and corrugated iron, which is noisy, hot in the summer and cold in the winter.

4) Make sure that roofs are very secure in order to withstand gale force winds.

5) Ideally there should be an overhang of approximately 1 m (3 ft) to give extra protection against the elements.

Flooring

Essential requirements:

1) It should be non-slippery, impervious to moisture, hard-wearing and must not strike cold.

2) A slope towards the rear of the stable of 1 in 60 allows fluids to run towards an external drain.

3) There should be an open drain, protected with a grid, outside the stable. The gutter leading to the drain should have a 1 in 40 slope.

The most common flooring is concrete, which is roughened to prevent slipping. A herringbone pattern set into the concrete aids drainage.

Cobblestones and stable bricks are sometimes used. They do, however, wear smooth and become slippery or uneven. Compressed chalk can be slippery if wet but otherwise fulfils all criteria.

A new form of flooring used in larger yards is the rubber matting or granilastic used in lorries. Granilastic is a rubber mixture which is laid and sets rather like concrete. These floors are laid on top of concrete and are expensive, but perfect for the job.

Doors

Stable doors should be 1.2 m (4 ft) wide and a minimum of 2.1 m (7 ft) high for a horse. The door should be in two halves, opening outwards. The top door should always be hooked open to allow in plenty of fresh air and enable the horse to see out. In fact top doors are so rarely closed that they may not be considered a necessity.

The bottom door should have a top bolt, preferably of the sort that a horse cannot undo and a kick bolt at the bottom. A strip of metal should cover the top of the bottom door to prevent chewing.

Fixtures and fittings

The general rule is that the fewer fixtures one has, the less likely the horse is to injure himself. There should be a tying-up ring just below the horse's eye level, and a ring for a haynet just above the horse's eye level. These rings must be firmly fitted onto the wall and should have weak links such as loops of baling twine for securing. Should the horse pull back the weak link must break; the ring must not come out of the wall or, worse still, bring some of the wall down with it.

If a fitted manger is to be used it must be durable, safe and easy to keep clean. The ideal position is in the corner on the same wall as the door, set at a height of approximately 1.1 m (3 ft 6 in). Never position mangers on the far wall as this entails walking past the hindquarters of a horse who has just been fed and could be dangerous.

Water buckets should be robust, made of heavy-duty rubber. Plastics tend to split and can be dangerous. Again, these should be positioned safely, not against a far wall.

Automatic watering systems are widely used. They are labour-saving but the main disadvantages are that the pipes may freeze in cold weather, they could get blocked by hay, food or droppings and one cannot gauge the amount of water the horse is drinking. Automatic bowls should not be so small that they discourage a horse from drinking his fill.

Lighting

1) All electric light fittings and wiring must be well maintained to minimize the fire risk.

2) Bulbs must be kept free of dust and cobwebs. They should be of the self contained, fully enclosed type, or else be protected with a wire mesh.

3) All wires and fittings must be safely positioned and protected, with approved casings, from vermin and damp as well as from inquisitive horses.

4) Ideally, stables should be naturally well lit. A second window in the wall opposite the door will provide extra light.

Ventilation

The object of ventilation is to change the air in the stable frequently, thus keeping it pure and germ-free. As the horse breathes he expels carbon dioxide into the air. As he stales, ammonia is excreted in the urine. The ammonia rises in the stable with the warm air. Obviously if this air is not replaced with fresh air, the stable will become warm and stuffy. Horses need a constant supply of clean air to enable them to work and resist disease. Stale air and a dusty atmosphere will affect the respiratory system, thus interfering with the horse's fitness. The ventilation should be such that there are six complete air changes every hour. Not less than $42\,m^3$ (1500 cubic ft) of air space should be available in each loose box.

The stable must not, however, feel draughty. A draught is a sharp current of air which strikes cold as it touches the skin. A horse standing in a draught will be cold — one who is perhaps a bit damp and warm from exercise is particularly prone to chills if standing around in a draughty stable or lorry.

Ventilation can be provided by the following means:

Stable door. The top door should always be open. It would only be closed in extreme weather conditions or when darkness is required, for example after an eye injury or while a horse is in shock. It may be necessary to close the top door if an excitable horse is threatening to jump out for some reason, although in this case a grille could be used.

Windows. Preferably on the same side as the door to prevent a cross current of air striking the horse on his back. Always protected with a mesh or grille, the top portion should open inwards to direct fresh air upwards, thus replacing the stale warm air. The Sheringham window is of this pattern.

Louvre boards. These are boards set at an angle, with a gap in between. The angle stops rain and snow from entering through the gaps. They are fitted into the ridge at the top of the wall to allow warm air to escape.

Ventilating cowls. A cowl and tube can be fitted into the roof. These are designed to create a vacuum as air passes over the upward slant or through a narrow slit. This causes the warm air in the stable to be drawn up and out through the tube.

Warmth

The horse must be kept warm through the use of extra rugs, blankets and stable bandages, never through keeping him in a warm and stuffy atmosphere. Should a sick horse need extra warmth, overhead infra-red lamps may be used. Care must be taken to ensure that the lamps do not touch the horse and that the wires are concealed safely.

BARN STABLING

One way of providing stabling is to use the method of barn stabling. This is very popular in America. A purpose built barn may be used or an existing building converted.

Each horse has his own loose box within the barn complex. 'Loddon boxes' are ready-made units which the manufacturers will fit to your own specification. Other manufacturers also provide this service.

When planning a barn conversion, great care must be taken to provide good ventilation because the horses share the same airspace. Ventilation cowls and tubes must be fitted into the roof.

The barns must be well lit, light and airy to provide a pleasant environment for the horses. Avoid doors which open into the central alleyway − it is normally easier to use sliding doors on rollers. There must be water points and two or more well equipped fire points in every barn.

The advantages of barn stabling are:

1) All stables are under one roof making work more convenient − everything is close to hand.

2) Staff and horses are protected from the elements whilst stable duties are performed.

3) Horses can see each other for companionship.

4) It is an economical method of stabling, especially if using an existing building.

5) Given good design, there is plenty of airspace, so improving the ventilation.

The disadvantages of barn stabling are:

1) The horses all share the same airspace which can lead to the spread of infectious diseases.

2) When shaking up straw bedding the dust will invade the airspace of all the other stables which would aggravate dust allergy in any sufferers.

3) Fire may spread rapidly through a barn. The central alleyway must never be the only means of exit. Ideally each box should have an external door to facilitate easy exit in the case of emergency.

4) Doorways and gangways must be wide enough to allow the horse to walk in and out of his stable easily, without banging his hips. Always keep the central alleyway free from obstructions, including horses.

5) If stable doors are positioned too close together horses may fight, particularly at meal times.

PLANNING THE STABLE YARD

It is not often that you have the opportunity to plan a yard from scratch. More often it is the adaptation of existing buildings that has to be planned out.

Points to consider when planning a yard include:

Finance. Obviously this matter will greatly influence what you will and will not be able to do. Obtain prices of materials and labour from as many different sources as possible. It is very surprising how the range of quotes you are likely to receive will vary. Seek recommendations.

Convenience. Horses are extremely labour-intensive animals to look after. You must, therefore, plan the yard to minimize the amount of walking backwards and forwards done by you and your staff.

Planning Permission. As previously mentioned, the local authority must be contacted.

Yard requirements

Gates and Access. The most important point to consider initially is that of access and security. Entrances must be large enough for delivery lorries, horseboxes and tractors with trailers.

Ideally driveways and gateways should not lead onto a very busy road or be on a bad corner, although sometimes this is unavoidable. It is always worth considering, in these cases, the possibilities of moving the entrance; this will require planning permission from the local authority.

The driveways should be as level and as well drained as possible. Tarmac or concrete is ideal but expensive. .

Entrances to the yard must have gates which are kept closed at all times. Yards should be fully enclosed to contain any horses who might get loose.

Storage Barns. The siting of barns large enough for hay and straw storage is of prime importance.

They must be accessible by lorry or tractor and trailer, but not so far away to make collecting hay and straw too time-consuming.

If the barns are a long way from the main yards, a regular trip can be made to collect enough hay and straw to last a week, provided that a suitable small store is available on the yard.

One advantage of the barns being away from the yard is that it reduces the fire hazard around the yard. However, always ensure adequate fire fighting equipment is available in even the remotest barn. Obviously a strict 'No Smoking' rule must always be enforced.

Indoor School. For a commercial yard to succeed it is almost essential to have the use of an indoor arena. The advantages speak for themselves; it is possible to continue schooling and teaching in all weathers, at any time, summer or winter.

The main disadvantages are of a financial nature, indoor schools being extremely expensive to build in the first instance.

With the help of a qualified architect, plans must be drawn up and presented to the local authority for planning approval. Experts on planning law can sometimes overcome local planning-officer objections.

The size and siting will depend on available finance, space and access. Commercial yards have to pay rates on all buildings in use as part of the business. This must be taken into consideration when planning for the indoor school as the larger the building, the larger the rates bill. However, for a commercial centre, the school must be big enough to be of practical use.

Quotes must be gathered for the costings of the working surface to be used in the school, the electric lighting system and any extras that may be required such as spectator galleries, judges' boxes and sprinkler systems.

Outdoor Arenas. Although cheaper than an indoor school, these are still expensive if properly constructed.

Arenas must always be sited on level ground, again with good access, preferably sheltered from prevailing winds and not too close to a busy road.

The most important point to consider is that of drainage. Most of the problems experienced with outdoor arenas are due to inadequate drainage. An arena constructed on sandy, well-draining soil will fare a lot better than one built on a clay base. It is a good investment to have the land drained by a professional company.

There are many surface materials available. The manufacturers are usually very keen to discuss requirements with a potential customer.

Stabling. Horses are happiest if able to see each other and watch the yard activities — as mentioned, the square layout is ideal.

The Tackroom. This must be centrally sited to avoid too much walking to and fro. In a very large yard, more than one tackroom may be needed. In the interests of security, the following points should be borne in mind:

1) It should preferably be brick-built for added security.

2) Windows are not necessary as light can be obtained artificially. If there are windows in the tackroom however, they should have reinforced glass and be securely protected with iron bars. The iron bars should be set into the brickwork and not just held in with a wooden frame, which can be easily removed by intruders.

3) The tackroom will need a sturdy door with strong locks. Many insurance companies specify the type of lock required in their policies. Failure to comply may invalidate claims.

4) Many tack thieves do not even attempt to break strong locks, they simply remove a few roofing tiles and cut through

one of the rafters to gain entry. Take this into consideration, especially if your tackroom is in a remote area.

5) Heating of some kind will be necessary to prevent the tack from getting damp. A sink with hot and cold running water is a great help when cleaning tack.

The Feed Store. This should be centrally sited and easily accessible for the feed deliveries. Other points to remember are:

1) The door should be kept securely shut at all times to keep out any escapee horse.

2) Vermin-proof feedbins must be used for all feedstuffs.

3) Keep the floor well swept to discourage vermin.

4) A plug point is necessary if you wish to use a linseed or barley boiler.

5) Running water is necessary for soaking sugar beet pulp and filling the linseed/barley boiler.

The Office. If running a commercial yard, an office and reception area will be necessary. They should be:

1) Centrally sited.

2) Well signposted — new clients must be able to locate the office easily.

3) Well built and secure to deter intruders.

4) Always tidy and well kept.

Male and female toilets with washing and changing facilities are essential.

Car Park. All commercial yards must have adequate parking facilities. For the convenience of the client, try to have a level, well-drained area with either a concrete or tarmac surface.

Isolation Box. This is necessary whenever a horse shows any sign of having an infectious or contagious ailment. Also, whenever a new horse comes to a yard, it is a wise precaution to keep him in isolation for the first week to see if he is carrying any infection, should there be any doubt, especially when a horse has been purchased from a sale, or imported.

Points to bear in mind when siting the isolation box are:

1) The isolation box should be well away from the main yard, preferably downwind to reduce the risk of airborne infections being transmitted. It is, however, desirable for the horse to be able to see others to prevent him from fretting.

2) An additional storage building will be needed near the isolation box so that all clothing, grooming kit, feed and utensils can be kept separately.

3) A disinfectant foot dip must be placed near the stable for use by anyone handling the isolated horse.

4) The isolation box should have its own muck heap.

Muck Heap. It is easy to build three breeze block walls to form a bunker to help contain the muck heap. There must be access for any large vehicle and tractor which may come to take the muck away. For the sake of convenience it must be fairly near the yard, preferably downwind. The path to the muck heap must be level and dry to ease the incessant pushing of heavy wheel-barrows. There must be adequate drainage which must not be allowed to get blocked.

Water Points. In some yards there may be automatic watering systems, which save labour. If automatic systems are not used, the more tap points there are, the better. Taps must not project dangerously into the yard. All pipes should be well insulated to give protection against freezing.

Drainage. Not only does adequate drainage help keep the yard clean and tidy; in freezing conditions it can minimize the chances of accidents. Factors for consideration are:

1) A slope in the concrete of 1 in 40 to a central drain will keep the yard free of surface water.

2) Other than this, the surface of the yard must be level to prevent water from collecting in puddles.

3) Drains should be located in all gutters, preferably beneath all taps.

4) All drains must be protected with a 'horse proof' grille.

5) Regular maintenance is extremely important to prevent drains from becoming blocked. One way to stop hay and straw blocking up drains is to attach a rolled up piece of wire chicken netting to a length of string. Lower it into the drain and tie to the protective grille. The netting will allow water to pass, whilst catching any straw that has got through the grille. Periodically the netting is pulled out and cleaned.

Fire Point. A fire point is essential in all yards. When applying for a riding school licence, one of the requirements is a prominently displayed and well equipped fire point.

The fire point should consist of:

1) At least two foam extinguishers suitable for an electrical fire.

2) At least two water extinguishers.

3) A hose, attached to a tap with good water pressure. (Pipes must be lagged to prevent freezing).

4) A large water tank — salt may be added to prevent it from freezing.

5) Several red buckets marked '**FIRE**', some of which must be filled with sand.

6) An axe.

7) An alarm bell or triangle.

8) A sign giving clear instructions as to the action to be taken in the event of fire.
   Information on the sign must include:
   a) The location of the two nearest telephones.
   b) The name and address of the premises so that a stranger could tell the emergency services. The instruction: Upon discovering a fire, sound the alarm loudly and call for help. Dial 999 and summon the Fire Brigade.

c) Actions to be taken regarding the safety of the horses. A
suggested guide would be:
Take all horses out of their stables, using headcollars
if there is time. Turn all horses and ponies out into
paddocks, outdoor arenas or indoor schools. Remove
those in immediate danger first. If there is not time to
put on headcollars, open the stable door and try to get
the horse out of the stable in any way that you can.
(Obviously this involves an additional risk as you then
have to round up loose horses later, but it is a risk that
you may have to take in order to save them. Sometimes
a frightened horse will only leave his stable if blindfolded;
this is done using a damp jacket or jumper.)
d) Actions to be taken regarding fighting the fire whilst
waiting for the emergency services: people should be
advised to fight the fire without endangering their safety.

Prevention is, of course, far more desirable than cure —
enforce a very strict **NO SMOKING** rule. Signs to this effect
must be clearly displayed around the yard.

In a large yard, more than one fire point will be needed. Fire
extinguishers should be placed at different points around the
yard, especially in and around barns. The advice of the local
Fire Prevention Officer should be sought.

Signs giving the action to be taken in the event of fire
are available from the British Horse Society offices which are
currently located at Stoneleigh, Warwickshire.

Yard organization

However well planned your yard may be, the most important
aspect is organization. Every part of the yard must be tidy and
well kept. Try to maintain the highest standards of turnout in
the appearance of both horses and staff.

Keep every building in a good state of repair. Stable yards all
tend to have 'corners' here and there where rubbish and building
debris seem to accumulate. Periodically clear out these corners,
mow all grass verges, rake all gravel, sweep out all the little
obscure areas of concrete that tend to be forgotten. Litter bins
must be situated around the yard and should be emptied regularly.

Obviously if the yard is well staffed, being organized is much easier. Even if you have the smallest private yard, try to maintain high standards at all times. You can be sure that on the day you leave the tackroom in a mess, the yard unswept and in a state of general disarray, this will be the day that a prospective client or your local business competitor walks into the yard to see you!

The topic of yard routines, organization and management is discussed in full detail in another book in this series, *The Horse: The Equestrian Business.*

2

THE HORSE AT GRASS

As previously mentioned, the domesticated horse has undergone a significant change in lifestyle from that of his forebears, spending much of his time stabled as opposed to wandering freely, grazing, sleeping and drinking at will.

In order to keep the horse mentally relaxed, as well as fit for the work that is required of him, it is desirable to strike a balance between the amount of time spent stabled and the time spent out at grass. As horsemasters we are constantly striving to provide the highest quality of care for the horse. This quality must not be limited to the confines of the loose box, but must extend out to the paddocks.

The advantages of keeping a horse at grass are:

1) The horse is able to exercise himself, so eliminating problems caused through insufficient exercise — such as filled legs — and general unruly behaviour.

2) It saves labour because there is no mucking out. Constant attention is not necessary.

3) The horse's natural desire to roam is fulfilled, thus keeping him mentally relaxed.

18

4) Money is saved on bedding materials, although a bedded-down shelter must be provided.

5) The horse will be less prone to coughs, colds and dust allergies.

The disadvantages of keeping a horse at grass are:

1) The horse will develop a thick, greasy coat and will, particularly in winter, normally be very dirty, making it more difficult to tidy him before riding.

2) If you wish to ride on a wet day, the horse will be wet and covered in mud. Wet mud around the legs can cause problems such as cracked heels and mud fever. The hooves also become softer if constantly wet so shoes must always be worn to prevent the horse from becoming footsore.

3) It is not possible to monitor the intake of grass or water. In the spring and summer the horse may become overweight, possibly suffering from laminitis.

4) It is not so easy to maintain and monitor fitness.

5) Unless a strict worming programme is adhered to, parasitic worm larvae will be ingested in quantity. In addition to affecting horses' health, this will also perpetuate the worms' life cycle and cause further spread of infestation. To assist in the control of infestation, droppings must be removed from fields regularly.

6) Paddocks will become badly poached in wet weather.

7) There is less security, especially if the field is away from the house or yard.

The combined system, mentioned earlier, offers the 'best of both worlds'. Keeping the horse partially stabled and partially out at grass enables you to enjoy the advantages of both. The horse is generally stabled at night in the winter or when the weather is bad. In the heat of summer the horse may be turned out at night.

THE FIELD

The size of field required depends on several factors:

1) The number of horses kept.

2) Whether the horses are partially stabled or out permanently.

3) The soil type.

4) The drainage of the land, whether natural or artificial.

5) The types and quality of the grasses.

6) Whether there are any boggy patches, poisonous trees, ponds etc. which will need to be fenced off.

7) Whether the paddocks are also used as riding and exercise areas.

The siting of fields is usually beyond the influence of the horse owner but ideally should be:

1) Near to the house or yard to provide security.

2) Well away from main roads.

3) As flat as possible. Fields on the side of hills put an extra strain on the horse's legs. Hilly fields do, however, have their advantages:
   a) Horses get more exercise moving up and down.
   b) Natural drainage tends to be downhill. If it is possible to put gates at the top of the hill, it will minimize poaching around them.

THE SOIL

Before you can begin to think about the maintenance and improvement of paddocks, it is essential to have an understanding of the various types of soil and their characteristics.

There are many different types of soil; each is a complex mixture of mineral particles, organic matter, air, water and decaying plant and animal debris.

Soil fertility is dependent upon:

1) Mineral composition and texture.

2) Content of the organic matter (humus).

3) Depth of soil.

4) Height of the water table.

5) Drainage characteristics.

Acid or alkaline

The level of acidity in the soil will determine the quality of the grasses grown and the ability of these grasses to acquire the vital minerals from the soil. If the grasses are lacking in various minerals, the horse's diet will also be deficient.

Acidity is measured on a pH scale. A pH of 7 is neutral, while lower numbers are acid and higher numbers, alkaline. All crops have an ideal pH level for maximum growth. In the case of grasses a pH of 6.5 − 6.8 is about right.

Soils can be tested by the local Agricultural Advisory Service or a fertilizer company. Kits which enable you to test the soil and gauge the approximate pH yourself are available from garden centres.

Excessive acidity can be corrected through the application of ground calcium carbonate (lime). As an approximate guide, sandy soils, which have a tendency to be acidic, need liming every four years. Clay soils tend to be alkaline and need liming roughly every seven years.

Soil types

Soils are a composition of coarse and fine sands, silt, clay and humus. The name given to the soil depends on the predominant particle. The three main types of soil are sand, medium loam and clay. The types and percentages of different particles present in soil depend upon the parent rock upon which the soil lies. Soils upon a bed of chalk and limestone contain natural lime (calcium carbonate). The nature of the subsoil must also be taken into consideration when discussing soil types, particularly on the aspect of drainage.

Sandy soils drain easily, thus calcium which neutralizes acidity is washed through the sand and lost. Nitrogen is also lost very easily. Being light soils, they dry out earlier in the year than other types.

Loam soils range from sandy loams through medium to clay loams and are the commonest soil types.

Clay soils are classed as 'heavy' soils, with a tendency to be alkaline. They readily become waterlogged and are unsuitable for arable uses because the machinery cannot get onto the land. Clay soils are well suited to permanent pasture. As these soils hold water they are rich in nutrients but poorly supplied with oxygen.

Peaty soils are very high in organic matter, often waterlogged and have a tendency to be acidic. Their boggyness makes them unsuitable for pasture: extensive drainage is necessary in order to make use of peat.

THE IMPORTANCE OF DRAINAGE

Well-drained soil allows oxygen to mix within the soil particles. This helps root growth and the breakdown of organic matter, thus releasing nutrients into the soil. Grass will grow stronger and earlier in well-drained soil which warms up more quickly.

The method of drainage employed in any field will depend upon:

The natural drainage.

The level of the ground water table.

The type of topsoil.

Nature of the subsoil.

The nature of the land, for example whether flat or sloping.

Drainage ditches

These must be checked regularly for blockages. The ditches on your neighbour's land must also be clear to allow the free run of water.

If putting in new ditches ensure that the soil is not dumped along the edge. Spread it out to prevent it being washed down into the ditch.

Ditches must always be safely fenced off to prevent animals from becoming trapped. Particular care must be taken to ensure foals and small ponies cannot roll under the fence and down into the ditch.

Keep all pipes leading to and from ditches in a good state of repair.

Underground drainage

When you are considering drainage of paddocks, the advice of a drainage specialist must be sought. A consultant from the British Institute of Agricultural Consultants may be able to help, or ask a local farmer who may be willing to offer advice as to which method of drainage is most suitable for the land in his area.

The use of underground pipes is always expensive, but the investment is very worthwhile because the quality of the land is greatly improved. When laying pipes underground the main systems are:

The parallel grid system. This system is used on relatively flat land, with pipes laid parallel to each other leading into either a mains pipe or ditch. The pipes are laid at depths of between 80 and 100 cm with a slope of 1 in 400 to the mains pipe or ditch. The spacing of the pipes will depend on the rate of water removal required.

The size of pipe used must be sufficient to carry off the water without running under pressure. A common size of pipe is 100 mm (4 in), made of either clay or plastic. The pipe sides are dotted with small holes, through which the water enters.

Once the pipes are laid in the trench, gravel or a similar

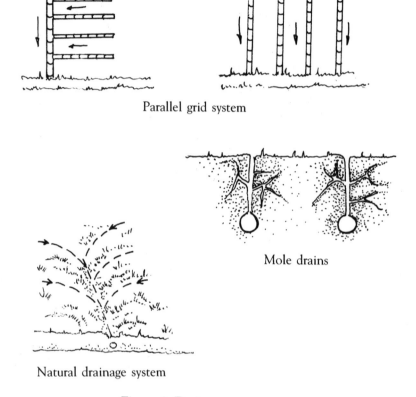

Parallel grid system

Mole drains

Natural drainage system

Figure 2 Drainage systems

substance is used to infill, thus ensuring a free flow of water downwards to the pipes. This permeable infill also has the advantages of benefiting from mole draining and subsoil treatments, ensuring that the pipes are effective for many years.

The natural pipe system. Here the natural lie of the land is used, with the pipes being laid down to follow the downward contours of the field. Pipes all lead to a main drain or ditch.

Mole drains. These are unlined channels which are created in the soil by a conical 'mole' which is approximately 80 mm (3½ in) in diameter. A mole plough is used behind a tractor.

Mole drains are used in the heavier clay soils and are effective for five to fifteen years. The presence of sand or drought conditions shortens the life of the channels.

The recommended depth for mole drains is approximately 525 mm (21 in), spaced 2−3 m (7−10½ ft) apart. The channels should either slope towards a main drain or ditch, or travel through the soil at right angles to any underground pipes present. If the soil is very clayey and therefore impermeable, mole drains across the lie of pipes will encourage the flow of water down through the permeable infill into the pipes and away via the main drain pipe or ditch. Care must be taken when using a mole plough not to damage existing pipes.

Subsoiling. This is the term used to describe the process of breaking up the subsoil to aid the water flow into the drains, as well as improving aeration.

Subsoiling must be carried out in dry conditions and will cause the surface to be very unlevel. Land will need to be levelled before the horses are turned out or before any other machinery can be used on the field.

SOIL DEFICIENCIES AND THEIR CORRECTION

The quality and feed value of grasses grown on a paddock is dependent upon the right balance of nutrients being present in the soil.

These nutrients include:

Nitrogen (N2)
Phosphorus (P)
Potassium (K)
Calcium (Ca).

Nitrogen is washed through the soil by rain so is mainly added in the growing season. Clover supplies nitrogen to the soil through the activities of bacteria present in nodules on the roots. These bacteria can convert atmospheric nitrogen into organic nitrogen compounds.

Phosphorus is necessary to ensure good root development. This can be applied in the form of phosphates, subject to the findings of a soil analysis. Phosphate promotes clover which is beneficial owing to the nitrogen production of clover roots. However, too much clover makes the pasture too protein-rich for horses.

Moreover, ingesting too much phosphorus inhibits the horse's ability to utilize the calcium in his diet. Therefore horse pasture must not be overdosed with quick-acting phosphate.

Potassium is usually present in higher levels in clay and loam soils. It is released slowly from the clay and is needed at root level to promote good development and growth of the grass.

High levels of nitrogen will inhibit the release of potassium. Potash (salts derived from potassium) will have to be applied to land if hay crops are taken regularly.

Calcium levels are maintained through the application of lime (ground calcium carbonate). As previously discussed, lime reduces acidity thus enabling nitrogen, phosphorus and potassium to be released from the soil as well as increasing the breakdown of humus by soil bacteria.

Calcium is washed through light soils very quickly as the lime dissolves due to the carbonic acid present in the rain.

Soils that are high in calcium carbonate will have a pH of 7. Any extra calcium present is known as free calcium carbonate (FCC): soils rich in FCC are described as being calcareous and never need to be limed.

Once the soil has been tested for these major nutrients, deficiencies can be corrected through the application of fertilizers.

Fertilizers

Fertilizers may be divided into three categories:

Organic: produced from substances derived from living organisms.

Inorganic: produced from substances of mineral origin including metal carbonates.

Semi-organic: pellets or granules consisting of an organic base mixed with inorganic nutrients.

Organic fertilizers. These are produced from natural resources such as seaweed, manure, blood, hoof, bone and meat meal. They improve the soil structure by introducing more humus, thus enriching the soil. They are safe to apply to pasture because the nutrients are released slowly into the soil as the materials break down.

Farmyard manure (FYM) is an organic fertilizer containing nitrogen, phosphate and potash. Horse manure must not be used on horse paddocks as this exacerbates the problem of parasite (worm) control.

Inorganic fertilizers. There are many different types available. Compound fertilizers provide more than one nutrient while straight fertilizers provide one main nutrient, for example ICI's 'Nitram' provides ammonium nitrate (nitrogen).

On a compound fertilizer sack, reference is made to the NPK levels. For example 20:10:10 contains 20 units of N (nitrogen), 10 units of P (Phosphate) and 10 units of K (Potash).

The nitrogen present in fertilizers is often a natural by-product of coal gas in the form of ammonium sulphate. This does, however, have a tendency to increase soil acidity. Another form of nitrogen is ammonium nitrate which is very concentrated, containing the highest level of nitrogen in any type of straight fertilizer. It would not be suitable for horse grazing until the pasture had either had a hay crop taken or been grazed by cattle. Too much nitrogen makes the grass too rich and high in proteins for horses. For this reason the first hay crop should not be fed to horses.

Phosphates are salts or chemical compounds derived from phosphorus, many of which are obtained from rock sources. Water-soluble straight phosphates such as superphosphate or triple superphosphate are extremely quick acting and, as with the nitrates, are normally too concentrated for use on horse pasture.

Types of potash used as fertilizers include potassium chlorate (approximately 50 per cent potassium plus salt), sulphate of potash and potassium magnesium sulphate. The latter is approximately 35 per cent potash and is frequently used on land grazed by cattle as the magnesium is vital in the prevention of the fatal bovine disease 'grass staggers'. Potash fertilizers are most effective if drilled into root level.

At least three weeks must be allowed, preferably with several heavy rain showers, before horses are put back onto fertilized land.

Semi-organic fertilizers. These are preferable for the horse owner as they introduce the necessary nutrients into the soil slowly, whilst promoting soil micro-organisms.

The advantages are:

1) As the nutrients are released slowly, they are less prone to leaching than inorganic fertilizers, thus reducing wastage and expense.

2) The earthworm activity is increased due to the encouragement of soil micro-organisms. This improves aeration which results in the breakdown of humus.

3) These fertilizers come in pellet or granule form so can be easily broadcast either by machine or hand.

Once the fertilizer has been applied, the fields must be rested for at least a fortnight to allow for the breakdown of the pellets. Rain will speed up this process.

The qualities and types of compound semi-organic fertilizers used will depend upon the results of a soil test.

To prepare for semi-organic fertilization the field must be harrowed well to loosen the matted dead grass and soften the topsoil in preparation for the fertilizer. Damp conditions encourage the breakdown of the pellets.

Liming

Where it is necessary to neutralize acidity, lime can be applied in one of the following forms:

Ground limestone is the commonest source of calcium carbonate for pasture; it is easy to work with and has a high neutralizing value.

Ground chalk is slightly more expensive owing to the drying procedure used before grinding. This also has a high neutralizing value.

Shell sand is obtained from beaches rich in shell fragments. The fragments are a good source of calcium carbonate. When used locally this is a cheap method of liming.

Calcified seaweed is available in granules or powder and contains calcium, magnesium and twenty-five other trace elements and minerals. The seaweed is easily spread onto the land and grazing can carry on immediately.

Lime should be applied when the land is dry to allow the machinery on without cutting up the ground. The lime particles will also settle directly onto the soil and will not smear on the wet grass.

Keep the horses off the land until the rain has washed the lime in.

Harrowing will help to mix the lime into the soil as well as loosening dead grass and improving aeration.

GRASSES

The main characteristics needed by grass for horse pasture are:

Palatability. Grasses which are too stalky and coarse are not palatable enough for horses, although they may provide a good tough turf, helping to stop the soil being cut up.

Digestibility. There must be a balance between too much fibre, which is difficult to digest, and not enough, as in lush spring grass. A certain amount of fibre helps digestion and satisfies the appetite. Too much fibre will result in the horse having a grass belly as the micro-organisms in the gut take a long time to break down the woody stalks, resulting in a distended gut.

Grass mixtures

When deciding which grasses to use, take into account the heading dates, that is the times at which the grasses come into flower and are at their most nutritious.

Try to choose a mixture of early- and late-heading grasses to provide a good level of nutritional value throughout the spring and summer.

A seed mixture suitable for a paddock could be made up thus:

Two perennial ryegrass varieties to make up 50 per cent of the mixture. Suitable varieties include S23, Perma, Melle, Meltra and Petra. These are all late-heading types. Rye grasses grow well in rich soils, but decline after two or three years if the soil is not kept well fertilized.

Twenty-five per cent of the mixture should consist of two types of creeping red fescue, which is very productive, giving a good turf. Types vary in quality but the better ones are of good nutritional value.

The other 25 per cent of the mixture could consist of 5–10 per cent each of crested dog's tail, rough stalked meadow grass (suitable for wet land) and smooth stalked meadow grass (also known as Kentucky bluegrass), which is able to withstand drought.

In addition a small amount (up to 2 per cent) of wild white clover, which grows on any type of soil, enhances soil fertility due to the formation of nitrogen in the root nodules. Care must be taken that the clover does not take over the paddock.

As an approximate guide, 35 kg per hectare (30 lb per acre) are the quantities of seeds used. Obviously this figure will alter according to the type of seed mixture and existing grasses if over-sowing.

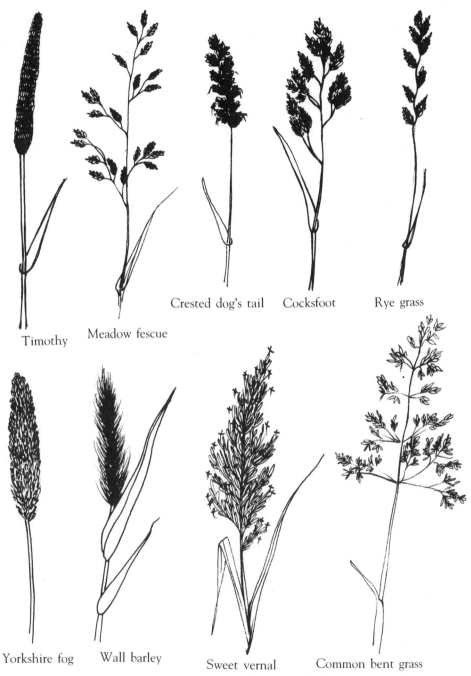

Crested dog's tail   Cocksfoot   Rye grass

Timothy   Meadow fescue

Yorkshire fog   Wall barley   Sweet vernal   Common bent grass

Figure 3 Grasses suitable (top row) and unsuitable (bottom row) for pasture

Other types of grasses which can be used in meadows include:

Timothy (S48). A persistent grass, useful in hay. Produces abundant amounts of seed and enjoys heavy loams and clay soils.

Cocksfoot. Hardwearing, suited to dry areas.

Agrostis (Highland bent grass). Very hardwearing, useful in gateways and on fields used for exercise.

Grasses unsuitable for pasture include Yorkshire fog, wall barley, sweet vernal and common bent grass.

Pasture herbs

Herbs may be introduced in the paddock as a highly palatable means of supplying minerals to the horse. Their deep roots extract the minerals from the soil.

If you intend using a weedkiller (herbicide) on the paddock, then obviously the herbs must not be mixed in among the other grasses. A herb strip may be sown along a fence line. Herbs prefer infertile growing conditions, so do not add fertilizer to the herb strip.

Common palatable herbs include:

Burnet. A deep-rooted, drought-resistant herb.

Chicory. A fast-growing biennial with bright blue flowers. Grows well on gravelly, light soils and is very deep rooting.

Comfrey. Horses do not graze comfrey but find it extremely palatable once it is cut and slightly wilted. Each day, leaves may be cut and fed to the horses. It can either be fed chopped and mixed in a with a short feed or simply put into a haynet. Between 2 and 5 kg per day is usually sufficient. Comfrey is extremely rich in proteins and minerals and has long been valued as an aid to wound healing. It is also thought to ease the symptoms of arthritis.

Comfrey is very easy to grow. Simply propagate from root cuttings in any spare corner or patch of land. Loams and clay

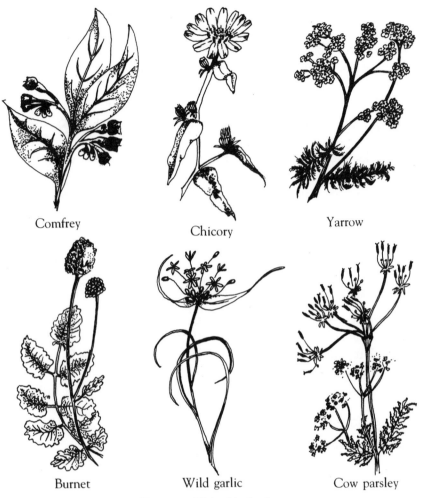

Comfrey   Chicory   Yarrow

Burnet   Wild garlic   Cow parsley

Figure 4 Valuable herbs

soils are best but they should be free of weeds. Sandy soils will
need to be improved through the use of organic manure before
the comfrey can be grown successfully.

Cow Parsley. Although horses enjoy eating cow parsley, it does
have a tendency to grow vigorously and spread over the pasture.

Wild Garlic. Many different varieties grow wild in the hedgerows.
Garlic is said to have many qualities, including that of fly

repellent and giving protection against colds and viruses.

Yarrow. Thrives on poor soils, is strongly scented with daisy-like flowers. Very deep rooted and loved by horses.

WEEDS AND POISONOUS PLANTS

Paddocks must be kept as free from weeds as possible, they have a tendency to take over the fields, using up valuable ground space and soil nutrients. Most weeds are unpalatable, indeed some are poisonous.

Any poisonous plants found in a field must be uprooted, removed from the field and burned.

The Injurious Weeds Order

This protective Act was made under the Corn Production Act of 1921 and the Weeds Act of 1959. Landowners are legally obliged to eradicate specific weeds from their land. Failure to do so may lead to a fine.

The following are covered by the Injurious Weeds Order:

Creeping Thistles and Spear Thistles. These must be sprayed in the early budding stage, before flowering in June.

Dock. Serious infestations must be sprayed in April or May and again in August or September.

Ragwort. Horses will not usually eat ragwort as it grows, it is more palatable in its wilted state and is deadly poisonous. It is particularly lethal when eaten in hay. Ragwort poisoning causes degeneration of the liver. 1−5 kg (2−10 lb) may be fatal.

Ideally ragwort should be uprooted, removed from the field and burned. This will have to be repeated every year, taking great care never to drop leaves on the ground. If a spray is used it must be applied while the flower is still in the 'rosette' stage as opposed to waiting for the flowering stem to appear. Never cut or mow ragwort because this promotes more vigorous growth.

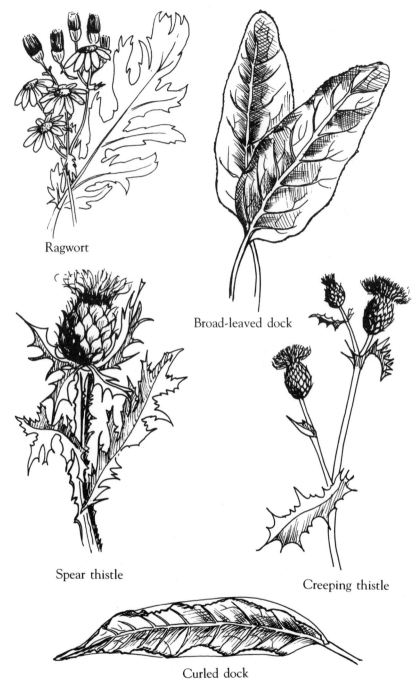

Ragwort

Broad-leaved dock

Spear thistle

Creeping thistle

Curled dock

Figure 5 Plants covered by the Injurious Weeds Order

Other types of weed

Buttercups. These are poisonous if eaten fresh, but are totally harmless when eaten in hay. In order to eradicate them, fertilize the soil to encourage strong grasses to smother the buttercups, then apply weedkiller. Large quantities would have to be eaten to affect the horse's health.

Chickweed. This smothering, fast growing weed is unpalatable and is best sprayed when in the seedling stage.

Nettles. Nettles are harmless if eaten, indeed some horses relish them if cut and allowed to wilt for a few hours. Nettles grow rapidly between April and September and should be sprayed during this time to eradicate them. Nettles soon spread and take over paddocks, so care must be taken to spray or cut them before they go to seed.

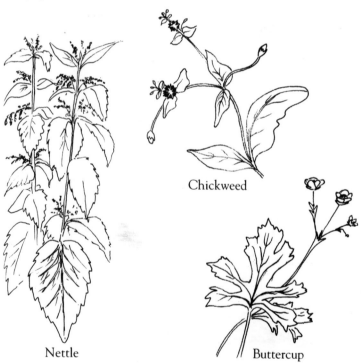

Chickweed

Nettle   Buttercup

Figure 6 Weeds

Poisonous plants

If a horse is suspected of having eaten poisonous herbage, the vet should be called immediately.

Other than those mentioned above, poisonous plants include:

Bracken. Normally horses will avoid eating bracken but on some commons and hills it is so abundant that quantities are ingested causing internal haemorrhages. The effects are caused through the cumulative build-up of the poisons. Bracken contains a vitamin B1 antagonist which results in poor growth, loss of condition and incoordination. Treatment includes the adminis- tration of large doses of B1.

Deadly Nightshade. Not normally fatal to horses although it can cause narcosis, dilation of the pupils and convulsions. The quan- tity needed to produce the symptoms depends on the animal's health and condition at the time of ingestion.

Foxglove. Horses will not usually eat fresh foxgloves although they are more palatable if eaten in the hay. A quantity as small as 100 g (¼ lb) will prove fatal. The symptoms of foxglove poisoning include contracted pupils, convulsions and difficulty breathing followed by death only hours later.

Hard Rush. Found in wet soils and very tough, usually only eaten if the rest of the pasture is bare. Hard rush should be sprayed and cut one month later.

Hemlock. Quantities of 2.5−5.0 kg (5−10 lb) of hemlock will prove fatal. Symptoms include narcosis and paralysis, with death occurring a few hours later.

Horsetails. Commonly found on wet soils. Large amounts eaten in hay are very dangerous. Poisoning shows as wasting and loss of control of the muscles. Horses will rarely eat the plant as it grows.

Laburnum. This tree is very common in gardens and quantities

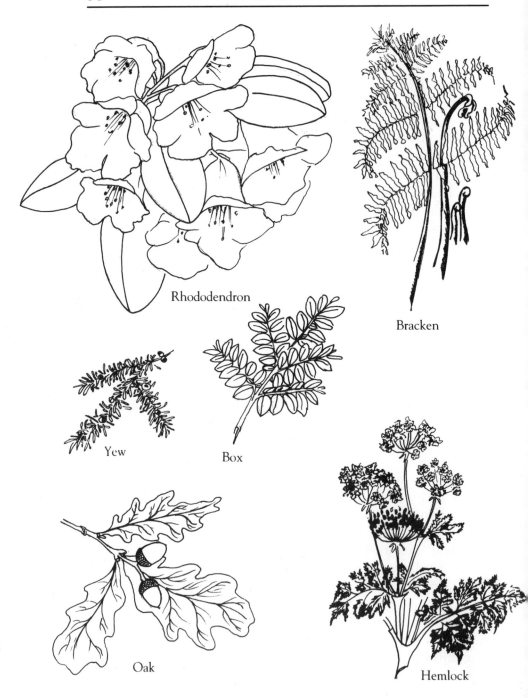

Rhododendron

Bracken

Yew

Box

Oak

Hemlock

Figure 7　Poisonous plants

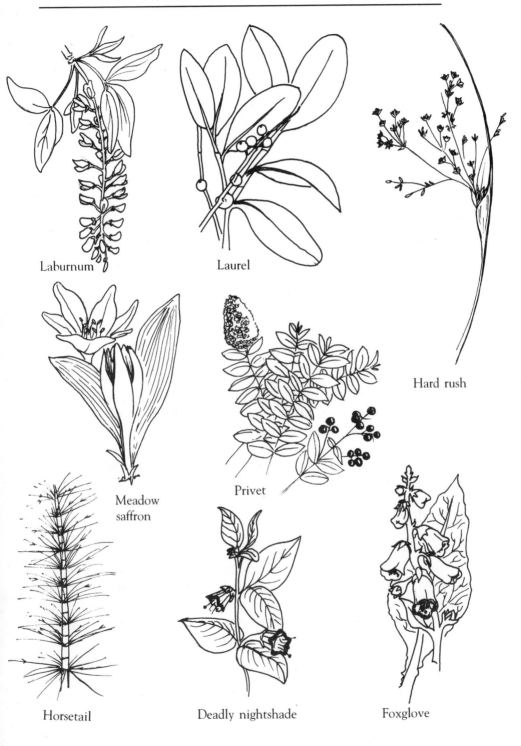

Laburnum

Laurel

Hard rush

Meadow
saffron

Privet

Horsetail

Deadly nightshade

Foxglove

as small as 0.5 kg (1 lb) will prove fatal. Although the whole tree is dangerous the seeds are the most toxic part. The symptoms of laburnum poisoning include convulsions and coma followed a few hours later by death.

Laurel. Usually found in gardens. Healthy animals can eat small quantities without it proving fatal. If, however, a 'poor' animal were to eat laurel, death would follow the laboured breathing and convulsions.

Meadow Saffron. This contains the poison colchinine which has a very marked toxic effect. The toxicity may take time to build up, by which time it is too late to save the horse.

Oak (Acorns). Acorns should be collected up once they have fallen because they can cause poisoning if eaten in large quantities. Pigs are often used to eat the acorns because they are not affected. The toxic effect of the acorns is not too marked; there is only a slight risk of poisoning.

Privet and Box. These hedges are common in gardens so again you have to be very careful that neighbours do not dump hedge clipping into your fields. Of the two, box is the more dangerous with small quantities causing death.

Rhododendron. The poison in rhododendrons causes death through failure of the respiratory system. Very small quantities are extremely toxic so care must be taken that all plants are well out of the reach of horses.

Yew. Yew trees are common in gardens, particularly for lining driveways. The fallen leaves and berries are as lethal as the fresh plant. Trees must be very well fenced off, bearing in mind that in strong winds, branches, leaves and berries may be blown into the field. A quantity as small as 0.5 kg (1 lb) is fatal. Horses will eat the leaves all year round, with the poisoning showing very quickly. The poison has a narcotic effect resulting in the horse falling into an insensitive state, similar to sleep. Beware that neighbours do not leave yew tree trimmings anywhere a horse may sample them.

Herbicides

When using any herbicide on pasture the most important point to remember is that horses must not be allowed to graze until heavy rainfall has washed all the weedkiller off the herbage.

The optimum time to spray pasture is when the grasses are still young. This gives the grass the best chance to grow strong and smother the wilting weeds.

On a small acreage, or for use on weed 'blackspots', a backpack spray kit is the most efficient means of spraying. Great care must be taken when handling weedkillers and the manufacturer's instructions on mixing and protective clothing must be followed exactly. Never spray on a windy day.

When spraying large areas, the advice and expertise of a contractor should be sought.

Herbicides must be stored in a safe place and any empty containers disposed of safely.

Most herbicides are hormone-based, supplemented with other active ingredients. A very useful type of herbicide is glyphosate which is manufactured and marketed under the name of 'Round Up'. Paraquat is also used (Gramoxone 100).

FENCING AND FIELD FIXTURES

The following factors must be considered when fencing paddocks:

1) Funds available — try to buy the best type of fencing materials that you can afford.

2) Fencing must be safe and non-injurious to horses.

3) The appearance of the fencing must enhance the fields and property, thus improving the overall value.

4) The fencing must be high enough to discourage horses from jumping out — approximately 1.5 m (4 ft 9 in) high.

5) The lower part of the fence must not be so low that a horse can put a foot over nor so high that a small pony or foal can roll beneath it.

6) Ideally all corners must be rounded off to prevent galloping horses running into the fence. Rounded corners also prevent bullied animals from becoming cornered in the event of a fight.

A windbreak can be incorporated into the corners by using slats of wood, made into panels approximately 2 m (6 ft 6 in) high.

7) With adjacent fields, leave a space between the fences if possible: this will prevent horses from fighting through the fence, but obviously increases the cost. The space in between can be used to plant a hedge which is useful as a windbreak, or to grow comfrey. The gap between fences can also be used imaginatively to provide a canter track and/or cross-country schooling fences.

Post and rail fencing

Ideally all posts and rails should be made from hardwood. A slightly cheaper combination of hard and soft woods may be used, but it is preferable to have hardwood posts.

The posts should be sunk at least 75 cm (2 ft 6 in) into the ground. Prior to sinking, the base of the posts must be treated with a preservative. The top of the posts should be cut on a slant to encourage rainwater to run off. Posts should be 2 m (6 ft 6 in) in length for a fence 1.2 m (4 ft) high and each rail should span three posts. The top rail should be level with the end of the post to lessen the risk of injury.

Half-round rails, two rails cut from one pole, may be used and although it does not look quite as smart, it is much cheaper than using square hardwood rails. Sawn rails must be a minimum of 75 × 38 mm (3 × 1½ in).

Post and rail fencing can be nailed together but nailing-on should always be done from the inside to prevent a horse from dislodging the rails by leaning on them. A more expensive method is that of mortising, whereby the rails are inserted into holes in the posts.

All wooden fencing must be treated with a non-toxic preservative. Creosote is commonly used, although tanalith is

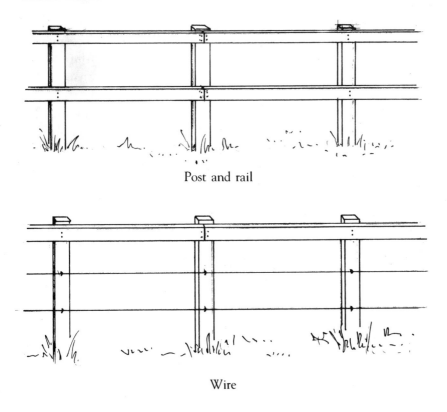

Post and rail

Wire

Figure 8 Types of fencing

becoming more popular. Tanalith does, however, contain salt which may encourage crib-biters.

There are several types of man-made fencing materials including a hardwearing nylon webbing called Flexafence which is nailed onto wooden posts. This form of fencing is completely safe although the majority of small ponies have no respect at all for it and will climb between strands. It is, therefore, best used in combination with a more solid form of fencing.

Wire fencing

Wire mesh fencing is only really safe when the openings are small and V-shaped. This prevents the horse from getting a foot caught. These fences are prone to stretching when leant on so may need to be supported with additional rails. This form of fencing is becoming increasingly popular, with more manufacturers advertising the product now than ever before. Mesh fencing is best erected by the manufacturer to ensure the correct tension, thus preventing sagging.

Plain wire fencing must really only be used to supplement a post and two rail fence, but if two strands are used there should be a visible top rail. The tension must be maintained at all times. Upright high tensile strands of wire known as droppers can be used to keep the wire strands correctly spaced.

Barbed wire is definitely unsuitable for use in horse paddocks and should never be used.

Electric fencing may be used to divide fields or to act as an extra fence to separate horses in adjacent fields. The wide-band electric strip fencing is suitable because it is more easily seen by the horse. Plastic strips cut from a fertilizer sack may be tied around the plain-wire electric fence so that a galloping horse can see it more easily.

Gates

When fixing gates the main points to bear in mind are:

1) Gates should be hung in such a way that they open and swing easily without scraping the ground or crashing open or shut.

2) The hanging posts must be substantial and set in concrete.

3) The gate must be of such a design that it is impossible for horses to get caught in it, and high enough to dissuade horses from jumping out.

4) Wooden gates must be treated with preservatives.

5) Put a chain and padlock around both ends of the gate to deter thieves and vandals from lifting it from its hinges.

6) Discourage people from climbing over or sitting on gates as this can cause the gate to drop and pull the hinges out of the gate post.

Shelter

Shelter must be provided as protection from:

1) Winds, especially of northeasterly origin.

2) Flies.

3) The heat of the sun.

4) Severe winter snows.

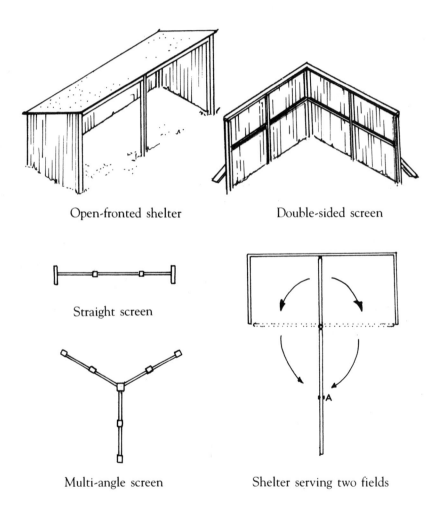

Open-fronted shelter   Double-sided screen

Straight screen

Multi-angle screen   Shelter serving two fields

Figure 9 Methods of providing shelter

It may be provided in the form of an open-fronted three-sided shelter which must always be southwest facing. The field shelter should sit on a concrete base which should extend out sufficiently to stop the ground from becoming poached.

Sectional buildings may usually be erected without planning permission unless they are of greater area than $30\,m^2$ (317 sq ft).

A multi-angle screen offers a good windbreak.

With careful planning a field shelter may be situated in such a way that it serves two paddocks. This would require two openings at the front, one of which would be kept closed off either with a panel gate or slip rails. Whichever gate was to be open would be hooked safely at A (see Figure 9).

Whichever design of field shelter is chosen, it is important that no horse can be bullied and trapped inside, so wide openings are necessary.

Watering arrangements

Watering requirements vary according to the time of year, temperature, lushness of the grass and whether the horses are in work or not.

The ideal method of providing water in the field is through the use of a self-filling trough. The trough should be:

1) Recessed into the fenceline to avoid too much of a projection.

2) Situated on a well-drained part of the field, preferably on a concrete pad to prevent poaching.

3) Situated away from trees or hedges because falling leaves would foul the water.

4) Free of jagged projections and easy to clean. The edges must be rounded and any taps or fittings safely boxed in.

5) Of a suitable height to prevent horses pawing at the water. Avoid any large gaps beneath the trough where a foal may become trapped.

If water is provided in buckets, ensure that they cannot be kicked over either by placing in car tyres or clipping the bucket handle safely to a fence post.

All stagnant ponds and sand- or clay-based streams should be safely fenced off. Remember that foals are notorious escape artists and could fall into a pond or stream and drown.

In the winter, ice must be broken three times daily. All pipes must be well lagged to prevent freezing. A plastic ball floating in a trough can prevent freezing-over except in very severe weather.

Feeding arrangements

When feeding in the field consider the following:

1) Timid animals may be bullied and give up their feed to the more dominant horse.

2) The feed and hay area will become very poached so, if possible, this area must be drained.

3) Empty haynets are dangerous so ensure that each net is tied high enough to prevent a horse putting a foot through.

4) Have more nets or piles of hay than there are horses to ensure everyone gets their fair share.

5) When choosing hay racks, always be sure that a horse could not catch a foot or in any way be trapped by the design.

6) Feed bowls must be of such a design that they cannot be kicked over.

7) Provide a salt and mineral lick to counter any deficiencies. This also helps to prevent horses stripping bark from trees. Mineral blocks should ideally be placed under cover to give protection against the elements.
Feed supplement blocks are very beneficial in the winter. They consist of a balance of all mineral dietary requirements in block form. The consumption of these feed blocks is often affected by the immediate availability of water, so to prevent a greedy animal from literally eating the block, keep it a good distance away from the water trough.

AN OVERVIEW OF PASTURE MANAGEMENT

The feed value and usefulness of any paddock can be maintained at a high standard with correct and careful pasture management. As we have seen, the main preconditions for good pasture are:

Adequate drainage.

Soil analysis and correction of deficiencies.

A sward of useful and palatable grasses.

Total eradication of injurious weeds and poisonous plants.

Having gone to the trouble of ensuring that the pasture is of a good quality, one must then carry out a management plan.

Division of fields

As we have established, there are several factors affecting the acreage needed. However, as a guide, the area required would be 0.5–1.5 ha (1½–4 acres) per horse. (1 hectare = 2.4711 acres, 1 acre = 0.4047 hectares [ha].)

This area should be divided up to allow for:

The resting of paddocks for recovery.

Fertilization and liming applications.

A hay crop to be taken if desired.

In the winter, use only one paddock for turn out, preferably the best drained. This ensures that the rest of the paddocks do not become poached.

Parasite control

All horses have, to a lesser or greater degree, a worm burden. This will be kept at a controlled level through a combination of good pasture management and chemical control with anthelmintics, administered to the horse.

The complete life cycle of the various types of worms is discussed in full detail later in this book. However, a brief description of the reproductive process of the large redworm (Strongylus vulgaris) will help to show why good pasture management is so important. The female worm lays eggs in the horse's intestines; these eggs are then passed out in the droppings. In warm, moist conditions the eggs hatch into larvae that crawl onto the blades of grass to await ingestion. Once eaten, the larvae burrow into the gut linings where some then grow into adult worms.

Collection of droppings is therefore very important since it helps to reduce the numbers of worm larvae that climb onto the grass stalks. To be totally effective this should be done daily or at least twice a week. This is possible for the one-horse owner on a small acreage or for the yard with sufficient staff. For larger establishments a specially designed paddock vacuum cleaner will save a lot of time.

Harrowing, carried out correctly, can also help control parasites. Harrowing must only be done in dry weather so that the droppings are spread over a wide area and dried out thoroughly, thus killing the worm eggs and larvae. Harrowing in moist conditions simply spreads the larvae around.

Regular harrowing is also beneficial to the pasture as it pulls up any dead matted grass, making room for new growth. It should also be carried out before fertilizing. Chain harrows may be dragged over the pasture either with a tractor or four-wheel drive vehicle.

Combined Grazing. Cattle and sheep may be used to tidy up the field by eating the rougher herbage left by horses. The worm larvae will also be destroyed within the cattle's digestive system. All fencing must be completely stockproof. Check that cattle are free from any form of contagious infection such as ringworm.

Topping. If grass gets long and rank it should be topped to a height of approximately 15 cm (6 in). Topping also helps to control worm larvae which may have crawled onto the stalks.

Weedy areas and brambles can be topped in an effort to eradicate them.

Pasture improvement

If confronted with a very poor, horse-sick paddock, one might contemplate ploughing it up and starting afresh. A local farmer would have to be contracted to do the work which will include ploughing, rotovating, harrowing and rolling to produce a good fine seed bed. He would then re-seed the following spring or autumn and fertilize. Sheep should graze the first sward as they are less likely to cut up the ground. Alternatively it can be topped.

This process is, however, rather drastic and renders the pasture unusable for at least a year, so is generally done only as a last resort. Usually, grassland can be improved immensely without going to the lengths of ploughing up.

The following programme would have dramatic effects on the quality of any pasture. Having removed the horses:

1) Ensure adequate drainage and clean out existing ditches.

2) Repair fencing and remove droppings.

3) Have soil tested and limed accordingly.

4) Destroy weeds with herbicide. Pull up and burn any poisonous plants.

5) Put cattle on to eat down rough grass and reduce worm larvae.

6) Harrow intensively.

7) Fertilize.

8) Seed using either machinery to direct drill or slot seed or broadcast by hand.

9) Roll to ensure seeds are well bedded.

10) Give the new grass time to become established, then top to encourage tillering (growth of the side stalks of grass).

11) Once the grass is established again it may be grazed by horses who have been wormed.

12) Avoid over-grazing, keep paddocks clean, fertilize and rest as appropriate.

Methods of seeding

Direct Drilling. A contractor will be used to direct drill. This has the advantage of not disturbing the soil and may be used on existing pasture. Fertilizer and slug pellets may be drilled into the soil with the seeds. This is an economic and efficient method of seeding, enabling the pasture to be back in use relatively quickly.

Slot Seeding. After spraying with a herbicide, a slot seeding machine cuts small slots in the soil and at the same time seed and a semi-organic fertilizer are dropped into the hole. The field is then rolled to cover up the holes which prevents the seed from being washed away by rainfall.

Broadcasting by Hand. Fields should be harrowed first to loosen up the soil surface. Both seed and fertilizer may be spread by hand. Wear gloves for protection against the skin irritants present in the fertilizer. When completed, the field should be harrowed and rolled.

Pasture management — a calendar

November—January:

1) Turn horses out on the best drained paddock only; save all other paddocks from poaching.

February—April:

1) Analyse soil to check pH. A pH of 6.5 is ideal. Lime will be needed every 3—6 years.

2) Harrow, fertilize, re-seed and roll.

3) Rest to establish new grass.

4) If a hay crop is to be taken, clean the pasture, eradicate weeds, fertilize and rest.

5) Treat wooden fencing with preservative.

May—July:

1) Repair and strengthen the fencing.

2) The first crop of hay may be ready in early June.

3) The ground should now be dry enough to allow any work requiring heavy machinery.

4) After taking hay, apply potassium-based fertilizer.

5) Keep all weeds under control.

August—October:

1) Periodically rest all paddocks and regularly remove droppings.

2) Harrowing may be carried out (in dry weather only).

3) In a good summer, a second hay crop may be taken.

4) Seeding as required.

5) Attend to drainage requirements.

Nitrates are not usually applied in the autumn owing to losses through leaching.

TAKING A HAY CROP

Before deciding to take a hay crop from your pastures the following points must be taken into consideration:

1) Do you have the use of the expensive machinery needed to cut, turn and bale the hay? If not, do you have a reliable local farmer who will cut, turn and bale the hay for you and, if so, how much will he charge?

2) Do you have sufficient acreage of good quality grasses to make the venture worthwhile?

3) Is the risk of poor weather at haymaking time (just as the grasses come into flower) worth taking?

4) Do you have a barn large enough to store all of the hay?

5) Will the remaining paddocks cope with all grazing requirements?

6) Taking account of these factors, is it more economical to feed your own hay rather than buy in?

Haymaking

If you decide to take a hay crop, grazing must cease from early March and fertilizers be applied in March or April: the types used will depend on the results of soil analysis and the general condition of the soil. Ensure that there are no weeds or poisonous plants present in the sward.

The quality of the hay taken will depend on the following factors.

In the growing stage:

1) Soil type.

2) Fertilizer treatments given, thus improving the levels of N, P and K.

3) Weed control.

4) The balance of nutrients and useful grasses.

5) Weather conditions.

At the cutting stage:

1) The stage of growth when cut — which should be as the grasses flower. In meadow hay (mixed grasses), not all of the grasses will flower at the same time.

2) Weather conditions — ideally should be warm with a gentle drying wind.

3) Method of harvesting.

At the drying stage:

1) Whether barn drying methods are used. If drying naturally, rain can spoil the crop.

2) If the hay has partially dried out and then receives a thorough soaking, many of the valuable trace elements, vitamins, minerals, nitrogenous compounds and soluble carbohydrates will be leached out, rendering the crop of very low feed value.

3) Turning frequently will assist drying and prevent the development of mould spores.

At the baling stage:

1) Hay must be 70–90 per cent dry when baled.

2) It must be baled relatively tightly to give good heavy bales.

3) Once baled the hay must be stacked and carted to a dry storage area.

Once in storage:

1) The hay must be completely dry, otherwise the stack will start to rot.

2) Also, if there is moisture still present, (higher than 10–30 per cent), micro-organisms will be actively inducing chemical changes within the stack. These chemical changes are heat producing which may result in the hay becoming 'mowburnt' (blackened and inedible). At worst the stack may overheat to such a degree that spontaneous combustion occurs.

The correct method of storing hay:

1) Prepare the barn – sweep out the floors and bring any older hay forwards to be used first.

2) Use wooden pallets on the floor as a base for your stack to prevent the bottom bales from moulding. This also ensures a free flow of air. Before covering the pallets with the hay, lay down rat poison on the floor.

3) Stack in such a way that you allow air to circulate to reduce the risk of overheating.

4) If stacking outside, great care must be taken with tarpaulins. They cause the hay to 'sweat' which will result in rotting. Use straw or old hay on the outside edges to help protect the valuable hay.

The use of preservatives

Recently the benefits of using chemical preservatives on hay have been realised. The preservatives are applied to the cut grass either before or during baling and will prevent moulds from developing. Most of the preservatives are based on pro-prionic acid or acetic acid. The main disadvantage of proprionic acid is that it destroys vitamin E, so whenever treated hay is fed, a vitamin supplement will be needed.

(Proprionic acid can also be found as a volatile fatty acid produced in the large intestine of the horse during the process of digestion.)

General notes on haymaking: a resumé

1) Hay made up of mixed grasses and clovers will come into flower at different times. Care must be taken to cut as the majority of grasses are coming into flower.

2) Clover has a higher moisture content than grasses, so will take longer to dry, possibly causing moulds to form. Once a hay crop has been taken, a reduction in growing clover will be noticed.

3) The later the hay crop is taken, the more fibrous the stems become, making the hay less digestible.

4) It is possible to get two cuts of hay from well-fertilized land that has a selection of high-production grasses.

5) Once the hay crop has been taken, potash should be applied to the land.

6) On well-fertilized land with a good intensive sward, one would expect, on average, a yield of approximately 5000 kg per hectare (2 tonnes per acre).

Silage

Any feedstuff which has been placed in a sealed container and encouraged to 'pickle in its own juices' is known as silage.

The crop is cut and bagged and, owing to the fact that air is present, bacteria producing lactic acid are able to work. Lactic acid is a volatile fatty acid (VFA) also found in the horse's intestine during the process of digestion. The carbohydrates present begin to ferment causing acidic conditions. The ideal pH is 4 and this level of acidity should be reached quickly in order to preserve the proteins and prevent the formation of the harmful butyric acid (another VFA).

The bacteria producing the lactic acid will be using up the oxygen. Once the oxygen is completely depleted the conditions are ideal for the action of butyric acid-producing bacteria. Butyric acid has the effect of breaking down the proteins into a toxic compound known as putrescine, resulting in a putrid smell as well as being poisonous if eaten. Furthermore, clostridial bacteria have been found to produce toxins causing botulism. This is why the very acidic levels must be reached as quickly as possible. The lactic acid will also break down proteins, but into a useful form of amino acids which are readily digestible.

It is normal to ensilage grasses only, as legumes (clover, alfalfa [lucerne]) contain organic acids which make it more difficult to achieve the necessary pH level as quickly as possible. If the crop is sealed and the correct pH level reached quickly, the feed quality should be good. If, however, the seal is damaged, air will enter and moulds and fungi will develop and spoil the silage.

Grass is cut for silage usually just after heading and is often treated with a preservative and allowed to wilt and dry slightly before being ensiled. The silage is often contained in sealed 'big bales' which are really only moveable with the use of machinery.

Horses must be introduced to silage very gradually and great care must be taken that it is in no way contaminated. If in any doubt, it is best avoided as a forage for horses.

Haylage

The grass used to produce haylage is cut between heading and flowering, allowed to dry partially and then vacuum packed into plastic bags. In order to ensure high feed quality and the correct pH for the preservation of the proteins, haylage is made mainly from rye grasses.

GENERAL CARE OF THE HORSE AT GRASS

1) Check the horses at least twice a day.

2) To increase security have the horse freeze marked, ask neighbours to let you know of any suspicious events or strangers in the field and keep both ends of the gate padlocked. Display signs to advertise the fact that your horse is freeze marked. Thieves are known to steal New Zealand rugs from the horse's back so mark these in some clearly visible way.

3) Remember the regular worming, shoeing, inoculations and teeth checks needed.

4) Check the horse's weight and condition. Increase or decrease short feeds and hay as necessary.

5) Check the horse for warmth in winter. Provide dry New Zealand rugs, plenty of food and a bedded down field shelter. Also remember that some thin-skinned horses will feel the cold on a cool summer night.

6) Check for the various ailments known to affect grass-kept horses and treat accordingly. These ailments include laminitis, sweet itch, mudfever and cracked heels.

7) Whatever the time of year, a constant supply of clean water must be available.

Finally, be observant. Learn what is normal behaviour for the group of horses in your care. Through constant observation you will soon notice when something is not right. Always check on your suspicions — the horse who stands apart from the herd ignoring the new hay feed may be suffering from colic. Don't assume that he just isn't hungry or is asleep!

3

NUTRITION

A balanced diet is essential to:

1) Sustain life.

2) Maintain condition.

3) Provide warmth.

4) Provide energy for maintenance and work.

5) Satisfy the appetite.

6) Provide the nutrients necessary for healthy growth.

THE NUTRIENTS

Each nutrient plays a vital role in the horse's well-being.

Carbohydrates are the main energy source. Energy is needed for all bodily functions including breathing, eating, moving, growing, pregnancy and lactation.

Lipids (fats and oils) provide a store of energy-yielding compounds and, as subcutaneous fat, prevent excessive heat loss from the body.

Proteins are essential for growth, repair and renewal of body tissues, health during pregnancy and lactation. Excessive dietary protein may be used as a secondary source of energy.

Water constitutes approximately 60 per cent of the horse's bodyweight. As with all animals water plays a vital part, performing several important functions.

Vitamins and minerals are essential for body functions. Deficiencies may show as clinical symptoms ranging from cracked hooves to infertility.

Carbohydrates

Carbohydrates are chemical substances found in plant and animal cells; their functions are to yield and store energy. They are formed by plants as a result of photosynthesis, the process whereby the plant uses the energy of the sun to create energy from carbon dioxide and water. This chemical energy is stored within the plant as one of the following:

Sugars. Monosaccharides or single sugars are the building blocks of the more complex carbohydrates. The most common single sugar is glucose.

Two single sugars may combine to form a disaccharide, for example glucose and fructose combined form sucrose; this is particularly abundant in sugar beet. Glucose and galactose combined form lactose which is found in milk.

Starch is the storage carbohydrate of all plants. Starch grains are abundant in the part of a plant concerned with storage; for example tubers such as potatoes and swedes act as starch stores for their respective plants. Roots and tubers consist of approximately 30 per cent starch whilst cereals contain roughly 10.5 per cent.

Cellulose. All plant cell walls are strengthened by carbohydrates called cellulose and lignin. In the wild, cellulose would provide the bulk of the horse's carbohydrate. Bulk or roughage is essential in every horse's diet to aid digestion. The stabled horse's cellulose requirements are met when hay is fed.

As plants get older their cells lignify (turn woody). As the amount of lignin increases the cells become more resistant to breakdown, becoming tough and indigestible.

Lipids (fats and oils)

Lipids are stored within the body as compounds of glycerol and fatty acids which contain carbon, hydrogen and oxygen. Glycerol and fatty acids are mainly stored as subcutaneous fat but a certain amount is held in the muscles and other tissues. The store of fat beneath the skin prevents excessive heat loss as well as providing a source of energy when needed.

It should be noted that carbohydrates can be readily converted to, and stored as, fat. Compared to carbohydrates, fats are a minor source of energy, especially as the horse's diet only contains around 4 per cent lipids. Lipids do, however, yield more energy per gram than carbohydrates − the utilization of this form of energy could be useful if trying to reduce the dependence upon carbohydrates as an energy source, for example to remedy or avoid problems such as azoturia and laminitis caused by too much carbohydrate.

Some fatty acids are essential − deficiencies of linoleic and linolenic acid can lead to growth impairment, failure of the reproductive system and kidneys, and skin lesions.

Proteins

Proteins are present within the body and in many different forms and are constructed of building blocks or sub-proteins known as amino acids. Twenty-three types of amino acid have been identified. Each is made up of a different combination of nitrogen, carbon, hydrogen, sulphur, phosphorus and oxygen.

All but ten of the amino acids can be synthesised in the body by micro-organisms from compounds derived from the metabolism of various food substances. These are known as nonessential amino acids. The other ten cannot be synthesised and must therefore be provided in the diet. They are known as essential amino acids.

The quality of a protein is determined by the number of essential amino acids present. Proteins containing all or most of the essential amino acids are said to be of high biological value (HBV proteins) whilst those lacking in all or many are of low biological value (LBV proteins).

Animal proteins such as those found in egg and milk are of high biological value, as are a few plant proteins such as those found in soya beans. The proteins in many cereals lack the essential amino acids and are, therefore, of low biological value. However, as horses are fundamentally herbivores HBV proteins should be sourced, where possible, from plant material.

The most important amino acids are lysine, methionine and trytophan, deficiencies of which will adversely affect protein synthesis resulting in impaired growth. All cereals are known to be low in lysine.

During digestion, proteins are absorbed as amino acids and used for growth, tissue repair and so on. For example, keratin is a fibrous protein used in the formation of hair and horn; collagen and elastin are connective tissue proteins.

Excessive nitrogen is removed by the kidneys and surplus protein broken down and stored as body tissue.

A certain amount of energy is derived from excess dietary protein, but only in abnormal circumstances, such as starvation, is tissue protein used as a source of energy.

Enzymes are always proteins; their function is to act as catalysts and speed up chemical reactions within the body.

Water

Approximately 60 per cent of the horse's bodyweight consists of water. The exact percentage is dependent on age and condition. Of this percentage two-thirds is found within the cells whilst the other third is in the plasma and digestive tract.

Functions of water within the body:

1) Helps maintain body temperature by cooling through the loss of excess heat in sweat.

2) Gives shape to the body cells.

3) Acts as a solvent in which substances can be dissolved and as a means of conveyance from one part of the body to another.

4) Provides a medium in which chemical reactions occur.

5) Provides a base for urine, thus aiding the excretion of waste.

6) Provides the base of milk for lactating mares.

7) Aids digestion.

Factors affecting water intake:

1) Diet, for example whether the horse is at grass or eating dry concentrates and hay. A horse on pasture may drink less due to the moisture content of the grass.

2) Temperature and environment: horses drink more in hot, humid conditions.

3) Amount and type of work. Sweating will make a horse thirsty.

4) Free access to salt and mineral blocks.

5) Health: the sick horse may be reluctant to drink.

As an approximate guide to the quantities of water consumed, a stabled large hunter would drink about 37 litres (8 gallons) daily.

Clean, fresh water must be available at all times. The only exception to this would be just before fast speed work. Change water frequently rather than just top up, because water becomes stale due to ammonia in the atmosphere.

Never remove the water from a horse about to do a long-distance event as dehydration is a serious problem. A hot, tired horse should only have sips of 'chilled' water (water that has had the chill taken off). Colic results if a hot, sweating horse takes a long drink of cold water. This can be severe and lead to shock.

A loss of 8 per cent of body water causes illness. Dehydration and heat stroke result from a loss of 15 per cent of body water.

Vitamins

Being required only in minute quantities vitamins are known as 'micronutrients'. Some vitamins are synthesised in the caecum by micro-organisms.

There are two categories of vitamins:

1) Fat-soluble vitamins which may be stored in the liver. These include A, D, E and K.

2) Water-soluble vitamins which may not be stored and include vitamins C and the B complex.

Fat-soluble vitamins

VITAMIN A. Also known as retinol.

Functions	By boosting the horse's immune system, helps resistance to disease. Promotes healthy bone and tissue growth and fertility. Improves night vision and the metabolism of fats and carbohydrates.
Sources	Green leaves, carrots, good quality hay, cod liver oil. The carotene present in green leaves is converted by the horse into vitamin A. Surplus vitamin A is stored in the liver. These stores may be exhausted over the winter; this is when cod liver oil may be given.
Deficiency Signs	Suppressed appetite, poor growth, loss of condition, increased susceptibility to respiratory infections, infertility, skin disorders and diarrhoea.

VITAMIN D. Also known as calciferol and the 'sunshine vitamin'.

Function	Aids the absorption of calcium and phosphorus in the gut, thus preventing bone defects.

Sources   Made under the skin by the horse when in sunlight.
                 Cod liver oil − necessary in the winter.
                 Colostrum provides rich source for the foal.

Deficiency   Swollen joints, skeletal defects and lameness.
Signs

Excessive quantities can lead to ossification of soft tissue.

VITAMIN E. Also known as tocopherol and the 'fertility vitamin'.

Functions   When in the presence of the mineral selenium, vitamin E aids the body's utilization of oxygen, thus improving stamina and performance.
                 Improves the muscle development.
                 Helps in conditions such as azoturia (tying up).
                 Improves fertility.
                 Reduces nervousness.

Sources   Fresh foods, grain, alfalfa and linseed oil.
                 Mares and stallions must have supplements of vitamin E early on in the breeding season. High performance horses need a supplement of vitamin E and selenium.

Deficiency   Poor performance, infertility, red blood cell
Signs   defects.
                 Degeneration of muscle tissue and, if combined with a selenium deficiency, liver damage may occur.

VITAMIN K. Also known as menaquinone.

Functions   Aids the clotting of blood and the metabolic uptake of cellulose.

Sources   Bacteria make the vitamin in the gut.
                 Green food.

Deficiency   Deficiency is rare. Some anticoagulant drugs will
Signs   interfere with the effects of the vitamin.

Water-soluble vitamins

VITAMIN B COMPLEX

B1 (THIAMINE)	Regulates the metabolism of carbohydrates.
Deficiency Signs	Deficiency is rare unless bracken, which contains a B1 antagonist, is eaten. Deficiency may lead to poor growth, loss of condition and incoordination.
B2 (RIBOFLAVIN OR LACTOFLAVIN)	Thought to have a quietening effect as it is important for the health of the nervous system and heart muscle tissue. Aids the metabolism of proteins and carbohydrates.
Deficiency Signs	Lower energy levels and poor growth and condition.
B6 (PYRIDOXINE)	Involved in the metabolism of fats, carbohydrates and proteins.
Deficiency Signs	Deficiency not common in horses.
NICOTINIC ACID (NIACIN)	Promotes healthy skin and aids metabolism.
Deficiency Signs	Deficiency not common in horses.
PANTOTHENIC ACID	Controls the metabolism of protein, carbohydrate and fats.
Deficiency Signs	Deficiency not common but would show as poor growth and condition.
FOLIC ACID	Prevents anaemia as it is vital to the production of red blood cells.
Deficiency Signs	Anaemia, poor growth and performance.

BIOTIN   Improves hoof wall structure, metabolism of fat, protein and carbohydrates. It is linked to the sulphur-based amino acid, methionine.

Deficiency Skin changes and poor hoof condition.
Signs

CHOLINE Aids fat transportation in the body and is a constituent of cartilage cells. Involved in nerve transmission and the maintenance of cell structure.

Deficiency Deficiencies are rare as it is widely found in feedstuffs and can be synthesised from the amino acid methionine.
Signs

B12 (COBALAMIN) Helps improve the appetite and the formation of red blood cells. Necessary for the utilization of protein, therefore promotes growth and aids reproductive processes.

Deficiency Anaemia, seen in youngsters more frequently than in mature horses.
Signs

Sources of Synthesised by bacteria in the gut. Grains, fresh the vitamin herbage, carrots, yeast, milk powder and soya B complex beans.

VITAMIN C (Ascorbic acid)

Functions   Prevents nosebleeds and aids the recovery from anaemia because it aids the utilization of iron.
Reduces stress and skin problems.
Fortifies the body's defence mechanism against disease.

Deficiency Since this vitamin is sourced as below, deficiency does not usually occur in horses.
Signs

Sources   Microbes synthesise the vitamin in the gut from dietary glucose.
Green leafy forage provides a useful source in spring and summer.

Minerals

Minerals may be divided into two categories:

Macrominerals, required in larger quantities, include calcium, phosphorus, sodium, chlorine, potassium, magnesium and sulphur.

Trace minerals, required in small quantities, include iron, copper, iodine, cobalt, manganese, zinc and selenium.

All plants contain minerals; the types and quantities depend upon the type of plant and the minerals present in the soil. Some soils are mineral deficient; this will be reflected in the quality of any feedstuff grown. *Although essential in traces, if fed in abnormally high quantities, certain trace minerals prove toxic.*

Macrominerals

CALCIUM (Ca)

Function	Promotes healthy bone growth, nerve and muscle function, lactation, blood coagulation.
Source	Limestone flour, grass, good hay, cereals (low), alfalfa and clover.
Deficiency Signs	Skeletal defects and increased blood clotting time.

PHOSPHORUS (P)

Function	Promotes healthy bone growth and energy production.
Source	Good hay, grass, cereals (high), especially bran.
Deficiency Signs	Skeletal defects and poor growth in youngsters.

These two minerals can only be utilized when they are present in the correct ratio and sufficient vitamin D is present.

It is essential for the horse's system to have a ratio of 2:1 calcium to phosphorus. Cereals tend to have a higher quantity of phosphorus than calcium. If too much phosphorus is present in the diet it will inhibit the uptake and utilization of calcium and therefore lead to symptoms of calcium deficiency. Especially when dealing with young growing horses, it is essential that, in the winter, calcium is added to the diet in the form of limestone flour along with a vitamin D supplement. Care must be taken when feeding bran because it is particularly high in phosphorus.

Ninety-nine per cent of calcium and 80 per cent of phosphorus present in a horse is contained in the bones. During the final term of pregnancy and during lactation, calcium and phosphorus intake should be increased to prevent these minerals being drawn from the mare's skeleton and to ensure healthy growth of the developing foetus.

SODIUM (Na) Most commonly sourced as sodium chloride (common salt)

Functions	Controls fluid balance within the body. Aids formation of blood. Aids digestion as it is necessary in making bile which aids the digestion of fats and carbohydrates.
Sources	Add 30 g (1 oz) common salt to the feeds daily. Provide a salt and mineral block.
Deficiency Signs	Sodium and potassium are both lost in sweat. A deficiency shows as fatigue — particularly after strenuous exercise — lack of appetite, slow digestion, constipation, poor growth.

POTASSIUM (K)

Functions	Osmotic regulation of body fluids, maintenance of pH levels (homeostasis), nerve and muscle function, metabolic uptake of carbohydrates.
Sources	All green plants and hay.
Deficiency Signs	Decreased growth rate and suppressed appetite, similar to sodium deficiency.

Dietary excess is excreted in the urine. Very high levels of potassium may interfere with the absorption of magnesium.

CHLORINE (Cl)

Functions	Necessary in the gastric juices for the digestion of protein and also for body fluid regulation and pH maintenance.
Sources	Chlorine is a non-metallic element found in many supplements and compound feeds.
Deficiency Signs	Deficiencies are unlikely, particularly when a mineral block is provided and/or concentrate cubes or coarse mix are fed.

MAGNESIUM (Mg)

Functions	Aids the formation of bone and teeth, is involved in all forms of energy production, nerve and muscle function, normal cell metabolism. Activates over 300 enzymes.
Sources	Most feedstuffs, particularly pulses, linseed, turnips, carrots, soya beans, alfalfa, good pasture and well made hay.
Deficiency Signs	Deficiencies may show as nervous tension and muscle spasms.

Trace minerals

IRON (Fe)

Functions	Promotes the production of red blood cells. Essential to the formation of haemoglobin which carries oxygen in the blood. Necessary for the functioning of the central nervous system.
Sources	Deep rooted herbs such as comfrey, and mineral blocks.
Deficiency Signs	A lack of iron may cause anaemia, particularly if aggravated by heavy worm infestation.

IODINE (I)

Function	Essential in the formation of thyoxine, the hormone governing the body's metabolic rate. Promotes growth and aids reproductive processes.
Sources	Herbs and seaweed, mineral licks, supplements.
Deficiency Signs	Cell abnormalities, poor condition, weak foals, suppressed growth and swelling of the thyroid gland. Excessive levels of iodine may prove toxic.

COBALT (Co)

Function	A component of the B12 vitamin which helps to prevent anaemia. Needed to promote bacterial activity necessary for digestion. Aids the synthesis of the B complex of vitamins. Activates enzyme reactions.
Sources	Fresh herbage, mineral blocks.
Deficiency Signs	Impaired B12 production which may lead to anaemia, weight loss and poor growth.

MANGANESE (Mn) AND ZINC (Zn)

Functions	Promote the healthy development of hair, skin and hooves. Activate enzymes necessary for digestion. Maintain a healthy appetite, coat pigmentation, fertility and normal cell metabolism.
Sources	Fresh herbage, good hay, cereals, minerals blocks, supplements.
Deficiency Signs	A lack of manganese can cause bone abnormalities and problems with the reproductive system. Zinc deficiency leads to suppressed appetite and reduced growth. Deficiencies of these minerals are rare as normal feed rations provide adequate quantities.

COPPER (Cu)

Functions	Bone, cartilage, elastin and hair formation. Promotes utilization of iron.
Sources	High levels in seed products such as linseed, and feedstuffs grown in soil containing the correct levels of copper.
Deficiency Signs	Depigmentation of the coat. Deficiencies are rare as normal feedstuffs provide adequate quantities.

SELENIUM (Se)

Function	When used in conjunction with vitamin E, considered to help prevent cell damage. Given to horses suffering or known to suffer from azoturia as implicated in *some* cases.
Sources	Fresh herbage, linseed and supplements. Vitamin E and selenium supplements are very useful for high performance horses, but should be given with care. Selenium is toxic in abnormal dosage.
Deficiency Signs	Weak foals, anaemia, joint abnormalities and, in some cases, azoturia. Excessive hair loss and hoof deformities are signs that the horse has ingested toxic levels of selenium.

Supplements

To ensure a good balance of vitamins and minerals in the diet:

1) Add 25−100 g (1−4 oz) common salt to one feed per day, depending on work rate, temperature and humidity.

2) Provide a salt and mineral block.

3) Grow a herb strip as discussed earlier. Herbs are very deep rooting and will draw up essential nutrients from the soil.

4) Compound feeds such as cubes and coarse mixes are specially blended to maintain constant and correct nutrient levels appropriate to need, being fortified with the necessary minerals, vitamins and trace elements.

5) Soil tests will show up deficiencies of particular minerals which can then be corrected by adding to the diet accordingly. Do this in consultation with a vet.

Supplements are available on the market covering the complete range of necessary vitamins and minerals. Some specialise in the provision of specific vitamins and minerals. Ingredients of the supplements may also include:

Yea-Sacc, a highly concentrated yeast culture which increases the digestibility of dry matter and fibre, increases nutrient availability so improving overall body, coat and hoof condition.

Amino acids; lysine, trytophan and methionine which are essential for the production of protein.

Supplements should be given after investigation has established a need for them, not ad lib or on a whim. Correct management and good feeding will minimize the need for supplements.

THE DIGESTIVE SYSTEM

It is the function of the digestive system to process all feedstuffs and assimilate as many nutrients as is possible from them. Having done this, all waste matter is excreted or egested from the body.

The carnivore gut is relatively short, but the herbivore gut is long because it deals with cellulose which is relatively difficult to digest and therefore needs to be held in the digestive tract for longer.

The equine digestive system consists of:

THE MOUTH
Contains:

Lips	Use to grasp the food.
Incisors	Cutting teeth used to bite the food.
Molars	Grinding teeth at the back of the jaw used to chew the food.
Mandibular, parotid and sublingual glands	These are arranged in pairs and produce saliva which warms, wets and lubricates the food to aid its movement down the digestive tract. Saliva is slightly alkaline and contains the enzyme salivary amylase which begins to break down starch.
Tongue	Forms the food into a bolus and passes the bolus to the back of the mouth.

THE PHARYNX (Throat)
The cavity behind the mouth through which food passes on its way to the oesophagus, passing over the tracheal opening which is protected by the epiglottis.

THE EPIGLOTTIS
A small cartilage at the root of the tongue which covers the windpipe (trachea) opening (glottis). This cartilage is depressed during swallowing to prevent food or water entering the trachea.

THE OESOPHAGUS
A tube approximately 1.2−1.5 m (4−5 ft) long which passes down the back of the trachea along the left hand side of the neck, down on through the chest between the lungs, through the diaphragm (a muscle which separates the chest from the abdomen) into the abdominal cavity and to the stomach. No digestion occurs within the oesophagus.

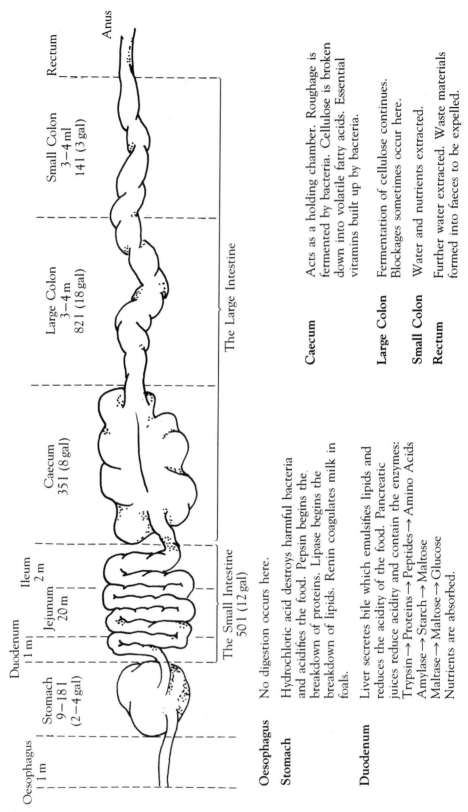

Oesophagus 1 m	No digestion occurs here.
Stomach 9–18 l (2–4 gal)	Hydrochloric acid destroys harmful bacteria and acidifies the food. Pepsin begins the breakdown of proteins. Lipase begins the breakdown of lipids. Renin coagulates milk in foals.
Duodenum 1 ml	Liver secretes bile which emulsifies lipids and reduces the acidity of the food. Pancreatic juices reduce acidity and contain the enzymes: Trypsin → Proteins → Peptides → Amino Acids Amylase → Starch → Maltose Maltase → Maltose → Glucose Nutrients are absorbed.
Caecum 35 l (8 gal)	Acts as a holding chamber. Roughage is fermented by bacteria. Cellulose is broken down into volatile fatty acids. Essential vitamins built up by bacteria.
Large Colon 82 l (18 gal)	Fermentation of cellulose continues. Blockages sometimes occur here.
Small Colon 14 l (3 gal)	Water and nutrients extracted.
Rectum	Further water extracted. Waste materials formed into faeces to be expelled.

The Small Intestine 50 l (12 gal)

The Large Intestine

Figure 10 Diagram to show the process of digestion

THE STOMACH

When empty the stomach is relatively small, approximately the size of a rugby ball, but it can expand to contain 9−18 litres (2−4 gallons). Food is allowed into the stomach by a small ring muscle called the cardiac sphincter.

Glands in the stomach wall secrete gastric juices containing hydrochloric acid, pepsin, lipase and renin.

Hydrochloric acid acidifies the food, pepsin begins to break down protein and lipase starts the breakdown of lipids. In foals, renin coagulates milk.

The horse's stomach is designed to remain half full at all times, taking approximately 24 hours to empty.

Once the food is sufficiently acidic it leaves the stomach, regulated by another ring muscle, the pyloric sphincter, to enter the first section of the small intestine.

THE SMALL INTESTINE

Consists of:

The Duodenum

This is approximately 1 m (3 ft) long. Into it flows bile, secreted by the liver and pancreatic juices, secreted by the pancreas.

Bile emulsifies lipids, aiding absorption and renders the acidic stomach contents alkaline before they carry on down the digestive tract. Bile pigments colour the food matter brown.

As the horse is intended to be a continual feeder, with the gut being designed to cope with regular intakes of small quantities of food, he has no gall bladder for storing bile.

Pancreatic juice is alkaline, containing sodium bicarbonate which reduces the acidity of the food. Pancreatic juice also contains the enzymes:

Trypsin which breaks proteins down into peptides, then into amino acids.
Amylase which breaks starch down into maltose.
Maltase which breaks maltose down into glucose.

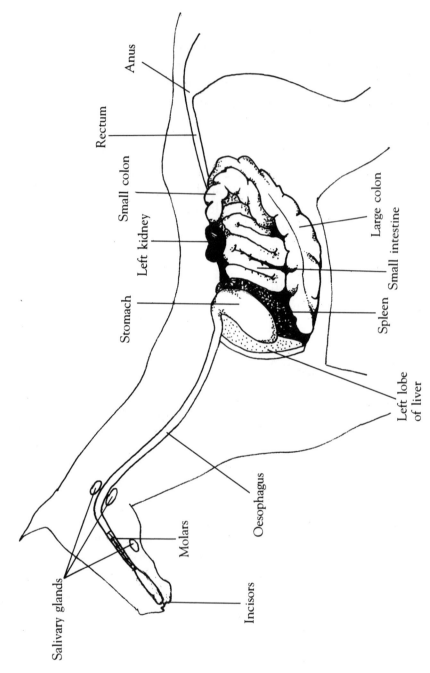

Figure 11 Location of the main digestive organs of the horse

Food is passed through the intestines by involuntary muscular contractions called peristalsis. The gut wall includes a layer of longitudinal muscle and a layer of circular muscle: these layers work antagonistically to push the food in one direction.

The Jejunum

This second part of the small intestine is approximately 20 m (66 ft) long. Along the intestinal walls are many small hair-like villi which give a huge surface area to aid absorption.

Amino acids, vitamins, minerals and glucose are absorbed into the bloodstream. Fatty acids and glycerol are taken up by the lymphatic system as minute globules and are transported to the vascular system which distributes the fat around the body.

Further digestive juices are secreted from the intestinal walls which aid the digestive process. These are neutral pH and contain the enzymes sucrase, maltase and lactase which convert carbohydrates into simple sugars, and erepsin which breaks proteins down into peptides and peptones.

The Ileum

The final part of the small intestine, approximately 2 m (6 ft) long. The food is now of a creamy consistency known as chyme, containing fibre which aids peristalsis.

The small intestine is held in loops by the peritoneum which folds around the intestines and attaches to the roof of the abdominal cavity — this is known as the mesentery. As well as supporting the intestines it supplies them with blood vessels and nerves.

The duodenum, jejunum and ileum have a volume capacity of approximately 50 litres (12 gallons).

THE LARGE INTESTINE
Consists of:
The Caecum
This is the first section of the large intestine and is capable of holding 35 litres (8 gallons). Food coming into the caecum is controlled by a valve. The caecum then holds food, passing it on a 'top-up' basis to the large colon.

The digestion of roughage begins in the caecum through the process of fermentation. This process is activated by a population of bacteria and protozoa specific to each particular type of feedstuff. Cellulose is broken down to release volatile fatty acids, a process which may take several days. The micro-organisms also synthesise essential vitamins.

A horse on a high roughage diet, such as one kept at grass, will have a large belly due to the bulk within the caecum.

The Large Colon
This is the second part of the large intestine. It is 3−4 m (9 ft 9 in−13 ft) long and holds approximately 82 litres (18 gallons). There are bacteria in the large colon which continue the fermentation of cellulose. The large colon has a sharp bend, turning back on itself, which is sometimes the site of blockages.

The Small Colon
The third and final part of the large intestine has a much reduced diameter and is 3−4 m long (9 ft 9 in−13 ft), but capable of holding only 14 litres (3 gallons). Water and nutrients are extracted through the walls of the small colon.

Further water is extracted in the rectum, where the waste materials are formed into faeces to be expelled through the anus.

4

FEEDSTUFFS

Feedstuffs may be divided into the following categories:

Cereals   These are the basis of the concentrate ration and include energy-giving foods such as oats, maize and barley. Cereals must be prepared in such a way as to improve digestibility. This includes boiling, rolling, bruising or heat treatments such as micronizing or gelatinizing. Food is gelatinized by intense pressure and heat treatment known as the 'dry extrusion method', making the starches much easier to digest.

Protein Feeds   Either of animal origin such as dried milk or of plant origin such as beans, peas and linseed.

Bulk Feeds   Bran, sugar beet pulp, grass meal and chaff.

Compound Feeds   These include the range of cubes and coarse feeds which are mixtures of the above.

Forages   Grass, silage, haylage and hay.

An understanding of the different nutritive values of the various feedstuffs will help when calculating a feed ration.

CEREALS

Oats have a high starch content, therefore they yield energy and can have a 'heating' effect. Good quality oats are plump, shiny, free of dust, pale yellow in colour and smell sweet. The oats are bruised to break the husk and improve digestibility. Once bruised, the feed value gradually decreases. Oats are at their most nutritious within three weeks of bruising.

Naked oats are a modern development of this traditional feed, the hull separates from the kernel during harvesting to leave a clean grain. Naked oats are more dense and have higher energy and protein levels than conventional oats. Fewer oats need to be fed to supply the same levels of energy in the diet and there is no need to crimp or roll naked oats. Naked oats are intended as a feed for performance horses. They can contain up to 27 per cent more energy than conventional oats, so great care must be taken when feeding them – they must be fed in smaller quantities, and the forage level of the diet must be kept up.

Good quality oats can comprise 90 per cent of the concentrate ration although they are low in the amino acids lysine and methionine and have a low calcium to phosphorus ratio.

Barley is less heating than oats although it is fattening due to its high energy content. Barley can make up 50 per cent of the concentrate ration, but no more owing to its relatively low fibre content.

Barley grains are rounder and plumper than oats with a clean and shiny appearance. It can be fed cooked and flaked or heat treated – micronized. Whole barley can be soaked and boiled to provide a nutritious, fattening feed.

Maize is a high energy feed containing little fibre. It is normally fed cooked and flaked and should be a bright golden colour, crisp and clean. Normally maize does not make up more than 25 per cent of the ration. If fed in too large a quantity it can cause an allergic reaction which shows as subcutaneous nodules.

Both maize and barley have a poor calcium to phosphorous ratio.

PROTEIN FEEDS

Linseed is the seed of the flax plant; small, flat, dark brown and shiny. Linseed is high in protein and fat, and therefore has a high energy value. In its raw state it contains prussic acid, which in large quantities is toxic to the horse. Therefore, always soak the seeds overnight. Change the water, bring to the boil and simmer for approximately one hour. The jelly and liquid can be separated if desired to make nourishing mashes.

Beans and peas are very 'heating', having a high protein and energy content. They may be fed crushed, split or micronized. Soya bean meal provides a rich source of high quality protein.

BULK (INTERMEDIATE) FEEDS

Bran is the offal from wheat and should appear broad, pink and sweet smelling in flakes. It has a low energy value and is ideal for horses in rest, acts as a bulk feed in the normal rations or may be used as a highly palatable laxative mash. The crude protein level of bran appears to be high but is not of a high quality or easily digested.

Once again the calcium to phosphorus ratio is poor so a calcium supplement such as limestone flour must be given.

Sugar Beet Pulp is a very useful non-heating and highly digestible source of energy and fibre. The sugar is instantly converted into energy whilst the fibre is fermented in the large intestine.

Sugar beet pulp helps to correct an imbalance in the calcium to phosphorus level caused by the feeding of cereals, as it has a very good calcium to phosphorus ratio itself.

Shredded sugar beet must be soaked in twice its weight of water for twelve hours; cubes for twenty-four hours in three times their weight of water.

Chaff consists of chopped hay which is often mixed with molasses to improve palatability. Other additives may include limestone flour, garlic and herbs. Chaff aids digestion and encourages the horse to chew his food more thoroughly and nutritionally it is a better 'mixer' than bran.

COMPOUND FEEDS

Concentrate cubes and coarse mixes come under the heading of compound feeds.

Concentrate cubes contain the normal short feed rations, maintaining a constant and correct nutrient level appropriate to the requirements of the horse. Cubes are specially blended and fortified with vitamins and minerals to suit the specific and differing needs of the various types of horse and include the following:

Complete cubes (Hi-fibre) also contain the forage and concentrate rations, so are very high in fibre. They are useful for a horse who is unable to eat hay, either due to an allergy or when hay is very expensive. They can tend to be boring and succulents should be fed in addition.

Horse and pony cubes are non-heating, palatable concentrates for animals in ordinary work.

Stud cubes are designed to meet the needs of brood mares, their foals, stallions and youngstock. They maintain condition and fertility through the inclusion of essential vitamins, minerals and trace elements. Particular emphasis is placed on adequate levels of calcium to optimize growth and bone development in the foal and young horse. They can also be useful for building up a horse in poor condition.

Yearling cubes are specially formulated to follow on from stud cubes, providing the nutrient density that is ideal for bone and muscle development and sound healthy growth. They contain calcium, phosphorus and lysine.

Racehorse cubes are designed to meet the needs of the high performance horse and contain high quality proteins rich in the amino acids lysine and methionine.

Event cubes are normally very similar to racehorse cubes with enhanced levels of proteins, vitamins and minerals. Both racehorse and event cubes must be guaranteed to be suitable for horses competing under FEI, BSJA and Jockey Club rules.

Protein concentrates are high protein pellets used in conjunction with other cereals and roughage.

Coarse mixes are designed to make up the whole concentrate ration to be fed with the normal forage. They contain a highly palatable mixture of cereals and bulk feeds with added protein, minerals and trace elements: mixes vary in their nutrient content. Horse and pony mixtures contain nuts, rolled oats, barley, maize, grass meal, molasses, linseed cake and bran. Higher protein mixes also contain protein cubes, peas and beans.

There are both advantages and disadvantages to compound feeds.

Advantages:

They are highly palatable and enjoyed by most horses, particularly the coarse mixes.

The quality of ingredients is guaranteed to be high.

The balance of nutrients is specific to the type of work each cube or mix is designed for. This makes it more difficult to over- or underfeed a particular nutrient.

Owing to the inclusion of vitamins and minerals, extra supplements will not be necessary.

Cubes have a long storage life, being more resistant to damp than cereals.

It is easier to measure out feed rations and saves on labour because no mixing is needed.

Disadvantages:

Some horses find cubes boring and go off their feed.

A sick horse may find cubes unpalatable and will probably not be tempted to try them.

It is not convenient to mix wormers or medicines in with the cubes.

Some non-heating coarse mixes may contain barley or similar cereals which can prove unsuitable for certain types of pony.

FORAGE

The horse in his natural state obtains virtually all his nutritional requirements from grasses. In order for the horse to perform and expend high levels of energy it is necessary to feed concentrates. It is important, however, to appreciate that the competition diet is an artificial one, thus great care must be taken when feeding. Wherever possible the horse's natural eating habits (grazing more or less continually) should be encouraged. Grass may be conserved although there will be some loss of nutrients during the process of conservation. Taking crops of hay, silage and haylage have been discussed earlier. To reiterate:

Meadow hay is a soft hay made from permanent pasture containing a mixture of grasses, normally low in protein.

Seed hay is a harder, coarse hay made from rye grass leys with higher protein levels.

Hay should be cut when the grasses are flowering. If left too late the seed heads ripen and are lost. 80 per cent of nutrients are in the leaf so stemmy hay is of lower feed value as well as being more fibrous and difficult to digest. Hay must be sweet smelling, mould-free and greenish in colour.

MINIMIZING DUST IN THE DIET

All hay contains a certain amount of dust. Contaminants include fungal spores, bacteria, pollens, dust mites and other dust fragments. Exposure to these harmful contaminants may cause obstructive pulmonary disease, respiratory hypersensitivity and infection. Steps must therefore be taken to minimize the horse's intake of dust to ensure good health and maximum performance. These steps include:

1) Soak the hay overnight to remove dust particles. Fungal spores will, however, survive the soaking so will still be ingested. Any dust particles which are not washed through will stick to the hay, which at least means they cannot escape into the air. The ingestion of dust and fungal spores would appear to be far less harmful than inhalation. A drawback with soaking is that nutritional value is decreased.

2) Steaming is more time-consuming and often difficult when using large quantities of hay. A large plastic dustbin may be used: pour boiling water onto the hay and replace the lid. Add boiling water periodically to keep the pressure of steam up.

3) Vacuuming the hay through a dust cure machine is the most effective means of removing contaminants. Having taken in the hay, it combs and vacuums it, delivering loose, clean material. The machine is fully portable but must be connected by a qualified electrician to a 20 amp single phase electricity supply. A mains water supply is also needed for a hose connection to the machine's exhaust.

   The machine is relatively expensive but would be an extremely valuable item of equipment in a large yard: in fact all horses and ponies would benefit greatly from the advantages of having 97 per cent of dust removed from their hay and straw. It should take about two-and-half minutes to process a bale but, in practice, the machine can prove rather more time-consuming.

4) Shaking up hay thoroughly using a long-handled fork out of doors allows dust fragments to be blown away. It is dangerous for the handlers to breath in large quantities of dust, as this can cause problems such as farmer's lung (hypersensitive pneumonitis), so a protective mask should be worn or steps taken to ensure that the dust blows away from the handler (but not towards horses!).

Haylage

A compromise between hay and silage. Rye grass is cut between heading and flowering, left to dry partially then baled and vacuum packed into tough plastic bags. When correctly processed the anaerobic storage conditions encourage the production of lactic acid which inhibits the activities of clostridial bacteria.

Haylage is very nutritious and highly palatable and must always be used within three days of opening a bale. Once the tough outer bag has been torn the haylage starts to deteriorate. One problem which may occur is that of boredom due to the smaller quantities needing to be fed.

The speed at which haylage is processed ensures minimal loss of nutrients and freedom from dust and fungal spores. So although it is fairly expensive, it is an ideal forage for horses in hard, fast work or any horse with an allergic respiratory problem.

Some manufacturers now produce a lower protein grade of haylage suitable for ponies and 'high fibre' bagged forage made from grasses which have been allowed to mature for longer resulting in more fibre and slightly less protein and energy.

Hydroponic grass

Hydroponic units allow grass to be grown in trays of water in specially heated and lit machines. This is a good way of providing fresh grass to horses, particularly in the winter. The grass is, however, very low in fibre so should not be used as the only forage feed.

Dried alfalfa

High quality alfalfa (lucerne) crops are harvested as near as is possible to the optimum nutritional stage, dried and specially cubed. Dried alfalfa provides energy and good quality protein. Dengie Dried Alfalfa have 16 per cent crude protein and 18 per cent crude protein feeds. Dried alfalfa may be used as the sole forage source to provide a dust-free ration if required.

Silage

Silage must be fed cautiously, introducing very small quantities at first. It is safest to avoid the use of big bale silage until more is known about the problems caused when eaten by horses.

ENERGY STORAGE AND UTILIZATION

Storing energy

The energy sources, in order of importance, are carbohydrates, lipids and proteins.

Carbohydrates are used first as a readily available energy source. Once this source is depleted, storage materials such as fat are called upon as necessary. Excess dietary protein cannot be stored so is either excreted or used immediately to supply energy, whereas tissue protein, that is, the meat of the animal, will only be used in extreme circumstances, notably starvation.

Carbohydrates are stored as glycogen — thousands of glucose molecules in long, branched chains — within the muscle cells and liver. The glycogen in the muscles is used as it is needed for work. The glycogen in the liver supplies glucose for all of the tissues of the body including nerve and blood cells. The glucose level in the blood must remain constant; this is controlled by the hormones insulin and glucagon secreted by the pancreas which direct the liver to release glucose as it is required. Excess carbohydrate in the diet can easily be converted to fat.

Fat is composed of triglyceride molecules — one molecule of glycerol to which three molecules of fatty acids are attached. Fat is stored within the cells throughout the body, in particular under the skin. This is referred to as subcutaneous fat or adipose tissue. The adipose tissue actually contains 30 times more energy than all of the glycogen within the body. A 'fat' horse is, however, at a disadvantage when working because more energy is needed to move the weight and the fat reduces the ability to lose heat. Therefore, an overweight horse creates a lot of heat in the production of energy but his cooling system is less effective.

The release of energy

Every activity performed by the cells requires energy.

Within every cell are high energy compounds called adenosine triphosphate or ATP. Each compound consists of a complex organic molecule of adenosine to which is attached a chain of three phosphate groups.

In the presence of the correct enzyme, one of the phosphate groups is broken off, an action which releases a large amount of free energy. Some of this energy is lost as heat but the remainder (mechanical energy) can be used directly for biological activities.

Once the energy has been released the ATP compound becomes ADP — adenosine diphosphate (adenosine to which are attached two phosphate groups). ADP then has to be regenerated back to ATP; this occurs quickly. The rate at which ATP is re-formed must correspond with the rate at which the original ATP is broken down to provide energy. Therefore the faster the horse is moving, the faster this regeneration must occur.

During tissue respiration sugars are broken down to provide the energy for the regeneration of ATP. Simplified, this occurs when a phosphate group is attached to the ADP.

This regeneration of ATP and the release of energy when ATP is converted to ADP takes place within the mitochondria, sausage-shaped structures referred to as the powerhouses of a cell. On average each cell contains about 1,000 mitochondria.

The rate at which sugar is broken down depends upon the amount of ATP being used up. Very little ATP is stored within the cell — the horse's metabolism ensures that it is regenerated at the same rate as it is needed. When this metabolism occurs in the presence of oxygen it is referred to as aerobic metabolism or respiration, the end products of which are carbon dioxide and water.

If the horse becomes short of oxygen, a certain amount of energy can be produced anaerobically, by anaerobic metabolism or respiration. This process is less efficient. The sugars are only partially broken down resulting in the production of less energy and a potentially harmful end product, lactic acid.

Anaerobic metabolism is a useful short-term means of energy production; when the lactic acid is oxygenated it is reconverted to sugars, any acid not reconverted being broken down and excreted. A problem can arise, however, as a build-up of lactic acid reduces the pH of the cell to an extent at which the cell becomes too acidic for ATP to be produced efficiently, which results in fatigue. The muscle fibres cannot contract properly and normal functioning is impaired. This is a major reason why horses should always be properly fit before being expected to work fast and hard.

Further information about respiration is given in another book in this series, *The Horse: Physiology*.

THE MAIN RULES OF FEEDING

1) Feed little and often.
   a) The horse's stomach is relatively small — approximately the size of a rugby ball.
   b) The horse is naturally intended to be a 'trickle feeder'.

2) Allow at least one and a half hours after feeding before working.
   a) A distended stomach will press on the diaphragm, preventing full inflation of the lungs.
   b) Digestion slows down during exercise due to the diversion of some of the blood supply from the gut to the muscles, resulting in a loss of nutrients and possibly colic.

3) Feed according to size, work, type, temperament, age and time of year.
   a) The bigger the horse, the more food is necessary for maintenance.
   b) A horse in hard work needs to be fed to provide the necessary energy.
   c) Different temperaments affect the choice between 'heating' and 'non-heating' feedstuffs. A naturally 'fizzy' type will require a less heating diet than a more staid, cobby sort.

4) Keep feed levels ahead of workload.
   a) Cut down on energy feeds the day before the rest day to prevent problems caused by an excess of carbohydrates in the system, for example azoturia and lymphangitis.
   b) Try to lead out in hand or turn out on rest day.

   c) In the event of unplanned rest, such as through lameness or extreme bad weather, cut out all energy feeds and replace with extra forage. Do not feed a lot of bran mashes because bran inhibits the horse's uptake of calcium. It is more sensible to feed a balanced ration of a non-heating compound feed such as horse and pony cubes.

   d) If fed energy-giving food, horses at rest will probably become less manageable and generally 'full of themselves'.

5) Water before feeding.

   a) Fresh, clean water must always be available except in some competition circumstances, such as before the cross-country phase of a horse trial.

   b) Should a thirsty horse take a long drink immediately after eating, food may be washed out of the stomach before the digestive juices secreted by the stomach lining are able to start the process of digestion. Many horses will take a few sips whilst eating; this is quite normal.

6) Feed plenty of roughage. There must never be less than 25 per cent roughage in the diet. The horse's intestine and caecum are specially designed to cope with a high roughage diet, containing many bacteria and protozoa which specialize in the fermentation of cellulose.

7) Introduce changes in the diet gradually. The bacteria in the gut are adept at fermenting and synthesising nutrients from specific types of feedstuffs. Therefore any sudden changes will result in impartial digestion due to a lack of a particular population of bacteria. This could result in a wastage of nutrients, diarrhoea and, possibly, colic.

8) Feed only good quality feedstuffs.

   a) Buy only good quality fodder and then ensure the best storage conditions.

   b) Store in dry, vermin-proof bins, always using up existing feed before adding newly opened feed.

   c) Some feedstuffs such as bran are prone to absorbing

moisture from the atmosphere. Purchase these in small quantities only.

   d) Keep all buckets, mangers and scoops scrupulously clean.

9) Feed something succulent every day.

   a) This helps to keep the stabled horse interested in his food and provides variety.

   b) It also provides a natural source of vitamins and minerals. Grass is an ideal green feed.

10) Keep to regular feed times.

   a) Horses enjoy a routine because they are creatures of habit.

   b) Whilst anticipating a feed, saliva is produced involuntarily in anticipation and readiness to begin digestion.

   c) It can be stressful to the horse if an expected feed does not arrive.

5

RATIONING

When calculating how much to feed, take into account whether feeding for maintenance or production.

Feeding for maintenance enables the horse's essential processes such as tissue repair, growth, digestion and respiration to occur without a loss of condition. Normally a horse can be maintained on a forage-only ration.

Feeding for production may be split into the following categories: growth; pregnancy; lactation; work; repair; fattening.

The horse requires energy-giving foods to ensure adequate glycogen in the muscles. If there is insufficient glycogen the horse will use the stores of body fat for energy, resulting in a loss of condition.

The digestible energy (DE) content of feedstuffs is measured in megajoules (MJ) (metric calories). It is necessary to know the nutritive values of different feedstuffs when calculating rations. Table 1 gives this information.

The nature of the horse's work will determine how much of the ration will be forage and how much will be concentrates.

Table 1 Comparative Nutritive Values of Various Feedstuffs

	Crude Protein %	Oil %	Fibre %	MJDE* Kg	Calcium %	Phosphorus %
Oats	11.0	5.0	12.0	14.0	0.1	0.4
Naked Oats	13.5	9.7	3.2	16.0	0.2	0.4
Barley	11.0	2.0	5.0	15.0	0.05	0.4
Maize	10.0	4.0	2.0	17.0	0.01	0.3
Soya Beans	50.0	1.0	6.0	17.0	0.25	0.6
Dried Milk	36.0	0.5	—	17.0	1.0	0.8
Linseed	26.0	39.0	6.0	27.0	0.3	0.6
Bran	17.0	4.0	12.0	12.0	0.8	3.0
Sugar Beet Pulp	10.0	0.5	15.0	14.0	0.6	0.07
Horse and Pony Cubes	10.0	3.5	8.0	10.0	Dependent upon manufacturer	
Racehorse Cubes	13.0	6.5	6.0	13.0	Dependent upon manufacturer	
Good Hay	10.0	1.6	32.0	10.0	0.4	0.25
Poor Hay	4.0	1.6	37.0	8.0	0.3	0.2
Haylage	16.0	2.5	30.0	11.0	0.4	0.25
Silage	15.0	4.0	30.0	12.0	0.65	0.35
Hydroponic Grass	16.0	4.0	14.0	17.0	—	—
Dried Alfalfa	15.0	1.6	30.0	11.0	1.4	0.2

* Megajoules of digestible energy.

Table 2 Ratios of Forage to Concentrates

Work type	Forage %	Concentrates %
Maintenance	80−100	20−0
Light Work/Slow Hacking	70	30
Schooling/Light Jumping	60	40
Medium Work	50	50
Hard Work	30−40	70−60
Very Fast Work	25	75

When calculating rations, common sense plays a large part. Constant observation of the horse's condition will help you to decide whether your horse is getting enough of the right sorts of feedstuffs to eat. There are, however, several steps which may be taken to ensure that the horse is receiving a fully balanced diet.

CALCULATING A FEED RATION

This involves ascertaining:

1) The horse's bodyweight.

2) The maximum amount of food a horse of this weight should be fed daily.

3) How much energy is needed daily for maintenance.

4) How much energy is needed daily for production.

5) The correct level of protein needed in the diet.

These calculations can be made using information provided and equations formulated by nutritional analysts.

The formulae may seem complicated at first glance but, if followed carefully and logically, it will be apparent how a balanced ration can be calculated.

Estimation of bodyweight

Bodyweight can be calculated or estimated in several ways:

Weighbridges. These provide an accurate way of finding out how much a horse weighs. Remember if using a commercial weighbridge that horses do not feel safe walking on sheet metal. To counteract this problem you could weigh the lorry or car and empty trailer first, then put the horse in and weigh again. Alternatively, place a sheet of rubber matting on the bridge.

Weighing machines specially designed for horses. Large yards, particularly those associated with racing, have use for them. Horses may be weighed before and after a race to assess the level of weight loss and stress.

Table of weights. A table of approximate bodyweights is given below:

Table 3 Approximate Bodyweights			
Type	Height (hh)	Approx. Weight Kg	lb
Pony	13.0	300	660
Large Pony	14.2	425	950
Small Hunter	15.2	500	1,100
Medium Hunter	16.0	575	1,250
Large Hunter	16.3	650	1,500
Draught/Shire	17.0	1,000	2,200

Weightapes. These are used around the girth and give the approximate bodyweight. They can be purchased from equestrian suppliers.

Girth and body length measurements. Measure around the girth (G) and from the point of shoulder to the point of hip (L) and use the following equations:

$$\frac{G(cm) \times G \times L(cm)}{8700} = \text{Bodyweight (kg)}$$

$$\frac{G(in) \times G \times L(in)}{241.3} = \text{Bodyweight (lb)}$$

Determining maximum daily feed

This is related to bodyweight.

A horse can only eat up to 2.5 per cent of his bodyweight daily, but does not have to eat to this maximum.

$$\frac{Bodyweight\ (kg)}{100} \times 2.5 = \text{Maximum daily amount of food (kg)}$$

For example, a 15.2 hh small hunter weighs approx. 500 kg as taken from weight table.

$$\frac{500}{100} \times 2.5 = 12.5\,\text{kg (28 lb)}$$

This means that 12.5 kg (28 lb) of hay and concentrates is fed per day, the ratio of which is determined by the sort of work the horse is doing.

Calculating energy needed daily for maintenance

The recognised formula is:

$$\left(\frac{Bodyweight\ (kg)}{10}\right) + 18 = \text{Daily Energy Requirements (MJDE)}$$

Example: 15.2 hh small hunter:

$$\left(\frac{500}{10}\right) + 18 = 68\ \text{MJDE per day}$$

Calculating energy needed for daily production

This depends to a certain extent upon what is to be produced.

Work requirements
For each 50 kg of bodyweight add the following MJDE:

Light work	One hour walking	+1	MJDE
	Walking and trotting	+2	MJDE
Medium work	Some cantering	+3	MJDE
	Jumping and Schooling	+4	MJDE
Hard work	Novice ODE	+5	MJDE
	Hunting once a week	+5	MJDE
	Hunting twice a week	+6	MJDE
Fast work	3DE	+7	MJDE
	Racing	+8	MJDE

Lactation requirements

First three months	+4½	MJDE
Next three months	+3½	MJDE

Pregnancy requirements
            Add 12 per cent for the final three months.

The formula used to calculate the MJDE required for a day's work is:

$$\frac{Bodyweight\ (kg)}{50} \times (\text{MJDE factor designated above})$$
= Daily work requirement

For example: 15.2 hh small hunter hunting once a week:

$$\frac{500\,kg}{50} \times 5\,MJDE = 50\,MJDE \text{ per day}$$

The total daily energy requirement can now be obtained by adding together the maintenance and production requirements.

To continue with the example of the 15.2 hh small hunter in hard work:

Maintenance	68 MJDE
Production	50 MJDE
Total daily energy requirement	118 MJDE

Ascertaining the correct protein level

First of all, it is necessary to know the crude protein levels required for various functions. These are shown below as percentages of total food requirement.

Table 4 Necessary Crude Protein Levels

Light/Medium Work	7.5–8.5%
Hard/Fast Work	9.5–10%
First three months lactation	14%
Next three months lactation	12%
Final third of pregnancy	11%
For growth:	
Suckling foal	17%
Weaned foal	15%
Yearling to eighteen months	13%
Eighteen months to two years	11%
Two to four years	10%

The levels of crude protein in feedstuffs are shown in Table 1.

Use the following table to calculate the percentage of crude protein in the feed ration of the 15.2 hh small hunter, estimated bodyweight 500 kg, in hard work with a crude protein requirements of 9.6 per cent:

Table 5 Feed Ration to Provide 9.6 per cent Crude Protein (CP)

Feedstuff	Amount of Feed (kg)	Content Crude Protein %	Protein in Ration (kg)
Average Hay	5.25	8	0.42
Sugar Beet Pulp	1.00	10	0.10
Horse and Pony Cubes	1.25	10	0.13
Oats	2.00	11	0.22
Barley	3.00	11	0.33
	12.50		1.20

1.2 as a percentage of 12.5: $\dfrac{1.2 \times 100}{12.5} = 9.6\%$

Thus this feed ration gives 9.6 per cent crude protein which is ideal for a horse in hard work. It also conforms to appropriate forage to concentrate ratios.

Example of a feed ration

To summarise these calculations, let us work through a fresh example from scratch. Imagine a nine-year-old 16.3 hh Irish Draught × Thoroughbred in hard and fast work competing in advanced one day events, aiming for a three day event. Temperamentally he can be 'hot' and as a result is prone to losing a little condition during training.

Planning the Ration:

1) Bodyweight, using table of weights = 650 kg

2) Maximum daily food intake (2.5 per cent of bodyweight)
$\dfrac{650}{100} \times 2.5 = 16.25\,\text{kg}$

3) Energy required for maintenance $\left(\dfrac{650}{10}\right) + 18 = 83\,\text{MJDE}$ daily

4) Energy for production: three day eventing $= +7\,\text{MJDE}$ per 50 kg bodyweight, therefore $\dfrac{650}{50} \times 7 = 91$

Total energy requirement $= 83 + 91 = 174\,\text{MJDE}$ daily

5) Protein requirement: between 9 per cent and 10 per cent is necessary for hard, fast work.

Using Table 2, a horse in fast work should receive 30 per cent energy from hay, 70 per cent from concentrates.

$$
\begin{array}{lrl}
\text{MJDE/day from hay} & 174 \times 0.30 = & 52 \\
\text{MJDE/day from concentrates} & 174 \times 0.70 = & 122 \\
\hline
& & 174\,\text{MJDE}
\end{array}
$$

Using Table 1, average hay contains 9 MJDE/kg

Therefore, 52 MJDE will be obtained from $\dfrac{52}{9} = 5.8\,\text{kg}$ hay per day

Oats and barley contain approximately the same amount of digestible energy; 15 MJDE/kg

Therefore, 122 MJDE will be obtained from $\dfrac{122}{15} = 8.13\,\text{kg}$

It will therefore be necessary to feed at least 8 kg of concentrates per day.

So 5.8 kg of average hay and 8 kg of concentrates would be fed per day. The additional 3 kg required to make up the total of 16.25 kg needed daily could be in the form of fillers such as Hi-fibre cubes, sugar beet pulp and possibly succulents such as carrots.

Slight downward adjustments in concentrates would be made if one were able to feed the best quality hay.

Table 6 Feed Ration Providing 9.85 per cent CP and 186 MJDE/Day

	Weight Fed per day kg	Crude Protein %	Approx. Weight CP kg	MJDE per kg	MJDE Fed
Average Hay	5.80	8	0.46	9	52
Sugar Beet Pulp	1.00	10	0.10	14	14
Oats	4.00	11	0.44	14	56
Barley	1.00	11	0.11	15	15
Horse and Pony Cubes	4.20	10	0.42	10	42
Linseed	0.25	26	0.07	27	7
Totals	(A) 16.25		(B) 1.60		186

Calculation of percentage protein in ration − (B) as a percentage of (A):

$$\frac{B \times 100}{A} = \frac{1.60 \times 100}{16.25} = 9.85\%, \text{ ideal for fast work}$$

Although the above represents 12 MJDE per day more than the calculation showed necessary, the energy content of all the above may vary depending on the quality of the feed.

The above feed plan fulfils all dietary requirements for the 16.3 hh eventer. A supplement of vitamins, minerals and salt would be added daily. It is necessary to feed linseed only twice weekly. The protein levels may be kept up in the remaining feeds through the use of HBV protein feeds such as beans and peas. The concentrate ration may be made up from oats, barley, racehorse or event cubes according to preference. Chaff may be used to improve mastication and to aid digestion.

Although feed values can be calculated mathematically and scientifically, there can never be a substitute for good old-fashioned common sense, bearing in mind the saying 'the eye of the master maketh the horse'.

The majority of horse owners feed through a 'feel' of what is right for their particular horse. By combining a few common sense points with the science of feeding, one can be assured of a well fed horse.

1) Always keep an eye on the condition of the horse. Is he losing weight or putting on too much?

   What condition do you want him in? For example, is he a show hunter or eventer? The show hunter will be required to carry more condition while the eventer should be free of superfluous fat. Increase or decrease feedstuffs accordingly.

2) Temperamentally, is he a 'hothead' or a calm, unflappable type? This will help you decide whether he needs a lot of energy feed or not. Many 'fizzy' horses event successfully on a low energy diet.

3) Does he seem to have too much or too little energy for the job required? A riding club dressage horse will not need to be as energetic as the eventer.

4) Environmental conditions will affect feed intake; in cold weather the horse will need warming feeds. In the spring and summer he may be out at grass so feed rations may be reduced if the grass is of good quality.

5) Adjust rations according to the horse's appetite, always making sure that he enjoys his food. Some horses are naturally good doers, while others tend to be poor. Check the teeth for sharp edges which may affect the ability to chew. Some fit competition horses go off their food during training. They may need variety or simply a rest from large quantities of energy feeds.

6) Finally, no amount of high quality food will keep a horse in good condition if he is suffering from a parasitic burden.

THE 'NON-SCIENTIFIC' METHOD OF CALCULATING FEED RATIONS

Feed rations are the subject everyone taking equestrian exams dreads. 'How much will you feed this horse?' The candidates' minds go blank — 'a scoop of this and a scoop of that' won't do. It has got to be in pounds or kilograms. No-one (or at least no-one I know!) could use the whole of the rationing formulae discussed earlier when being questioned about feeding in an exam situation. You do, however, need a formula to follow.

Useful measurements to remember are:

$1\,kg = 2.2\,lb\ (2\frac{1}{4}\,lb).$
$1\,lb = 0.45\,kg\ (nearly\ \frac{1}{2}\,kg).$

An average section of hay weighs approximately 1.8 kg (4 lb) When filled level, a normal 1500 ml (2½ pint) feed scoop holds the following:

1.35 kg (3 lb) cubes.

0.56 kg (1¼ lb) flaked barley

1.35 kg (3 lb) soaked sugar beet pulp.

0.33 kg (¾ lb) chaff.

0.67 kg (1½ lb) coarse mix.

1.35 kg (3 lb) carrots.

0.45 kg (1 lb) bran.

Maximum daily requirements calculated upon horse's weight:

Height hh	Approx. Weight kg			Daily food kg	Equivalent lb
12	250	$\frac{250}{100} \times 2.5$	=	6.25	13.75
13	300	$\frac{300}{100} \times 2.5$	=	7.5	16.5
14	400	$\frac{400}{100} \times 2.5$	=	10.0	22.0
15	450	$\frac{450}{100} \times 2.5$	=	11.25	25.0
16	575	$\frac{575}{100} \times 2.5$	=	14.3	31.5
17	650	$\frac{650}{100} \times 2.5$	=	16.25	36.0

Approximate daily feed for a horse in light work, based on a forage to short feed ratio of 60:40 (amounts shown below allow for adjustments to be made):

hh	Approx. daily amount kg	lb	60% Forage kg	lb	40% S/F kg	lb
12	5.4– 6.3	12–14	3.4–3.8	7.5– 8.5	2.0–2.5	4.5– 5.5
13	6.3– 7.2	14–16	3.8–4.3	8.5– 9.5	2.5–2.9	5.5– 6.5
14	8.1– 9.9	18–22	5.0–5.8	11.0–13.0	3.1–4.0	7.0– 9.0
15	9.9–11.25	22–25	5.8–6.75	13.0–15.0	4.0–4.5	9.0–10.0
16	12.6–14.4	28–32	7.6–8.5	17.0–19.0	5.0–5.8	11.0–13.0
17	14.4–16.2	32–36	8.5–9.6	19.0–21.5	5.8–6.5	13.0–14.5

When giving figures in exams it is acceptable to round up or down to the nearest half kg or lb so it is unnecessary to complicate matters by dealing in small fractions.

SAMPLE FEED CHARTS

Assume it is autumn and that all the grass has lost its feed value. The horses and ponies are turned out all day and stabled at night, except for the 16 hh and 17 hh who are stabled and fit for hunting and eventing. The others are in light work, ridden for approximately one hour a day and compete in unaffiliated competitions at the weekends. All are about eight years old, of a calm disposition and keep their condition fairly well.

There are many types of feedstuff to choose from — while those used in the following sample rations are suitable there may be other similar feeds which are equally suitable.

12 hh PONY

	kg	lb
Hay	3.2	7
S/F	2.2	5
Daily total	5.4	12.

Morning feed:

kg	lb	
0.45	1	Horse and pony cubes
0.225	½	Chaff
0.225	½	Sugar beet pulp
1.35	3	Hay in field
2.25	5	

Evening feed:

kg	lb	
0.45	1	Horse and pony cubes
0.225	½	Chaff
0.225	½	Sugar beet pulp
0.45	1	Carrots
1.8	4	Hay
3.15	7	

13 hh PONY

	kg	lb
Hay	4.5	10
S/F	2.7	6
Daily total	7.2	16

Morning feed:

kg	lb	
0.9	2	Horse and pony cubes
0.225	½	Chaff
0.225	½	Sugar beet pulp
1.8	4	Hay
3.15	7	

Evening feed:

kg	lb	
0.9	2	Horse and pony cubes
0.225	½	Chaff
0.225	½	Sugar beet pulp
2.70	6	Hay
4.05	9	

14 hh PONY

	kg	lb
Hay	5.8	13
S/F	3.6	8
Daily total	9.4	21

Morning feed:

kg	lb	
0.9	2.	Horse and pony cubes
0.225	½	Chaff
0.225	½	Sugar beet pulp
0.45	1	Flaked barley
1.8	4.	Hay in field
3.6	8	

Evening feed:

kg	lb	
0.9	2	Horse and pony cubes
0.225	½	Chaff
0.225	½	Sugar beet pulp
0.45	1	Flaked barley
4.00	9	Hay
5.80	13	

15 hh HORSE

	kg	lb
Hay	6.3	14
S/F	4.5	10
Daily total	10.8	24

Morning feed:

kg	lb	
0.225	½	Chaff
0.45	1	Sugar beet pulp
0.675	1½	Flaked barley
0.45	1	Horse and pony cubes
1.8	4	Hay in field
3.6	8	

Evening feed:

kg	lb	
0.225	½	Chaff
0.45	1	Sugar beet pulp
0.675	1½	Flaked barley
0.9	2	Horse and pony cubes
0.45	1	Carrots
4.5	10	Hay
7.2	16	

16 hh HORSE

Stabled most of the time, turned out for three hours daily, getting fit for BHS Novice Horse Trials. Slightly 'fizzy' nature and prone to losing condition.

	kg	lb
Hay	7.2	16
S/F	7.2	16
Daily total	14.4	32

Morning feed:

kg	lb	
0.225	½	Chaff
0.45	1	Sugar beet pulp
0.9	2	Horse and pony cubes
1.125	2½	Non-heating coarse mix
1.8	4	Hay
4.5	10	

Lunchtime feed:

kg	lb	
1.35	3	Horse and pony cubes
0.45	1	Carrots
1.8	4	Hay
3.6	8	

Evening feed:

kg	lb	
0.225	½	Chaff
0.45	1	Sugar beet pulp
1.125	2½	Horse and pony cubes
0.90	2	Flaked barley
3.6	8	Hay
6.3	14	

17 hh HUNTER

Hunting regularly, working at least 1½ hours daily to keep fit. 14 years old, prone to losing condition, particularly after hunting. Steady temperament.

	kg	lb
Hay	8.1	18
S/F	8.1	18
Daily total	16.2	36

Morning feed:

kg	lb	
0.225	½	Chaff
0.9	2	Oats
0.45	1	Flaked barley
0.45	1	Sugar beet pulp
0.675	1½	Coarse mix
1.35	3	Hay
4.05	9	

Lunchtime feed:

kg	lb	
0.45	1	Chaff
1.35	3	Oats
0.9	2	Sugar beet pulp
1.35	3	Hay
4.05	9	

Evening feed:

kg	lb	
0.225	½	Chaff
0.675	1½	Oats
0.9	2	Flaked barley
0.9	2	Boiled barley*
5.4	12	Hay
8.1	18	

* Boiled barley replaces sugar beet pulp for variety and helps keep weight on as this horse is prone to losing condition.

SUMMARY OF CRITERIA FOR RATIONING

When discussing feeding in an exam, remember that rations cannot be calculated purely on height and estimated weight. The following factors will all affect what and how much a horse will be fed:

1) Time of year − value in grass?

2) Whether turned out or stabled.

3) Work: hacking, eventing or hunting?

4) Ability to maintain condition; metabolic efficiency.

5) Temperament − calm or 'fizzy'?

6) Type: cobby or Thoroughbred? Light, medium or heavyweight?

7) Age − very young or old?

8) Susceptibility to conditions such as azoturia, laminitis.

9) Allergies.

10) Pregnancy and lactation.

Take into account all of the above points and memorize the daily amount each height of horse can be fed. This gives you a starting point.

Work out how much is to be hay and how you will divide it up. The remaining weight is short feed so needs to be allocated and divided up accordingly. Think in weight rather than in scoops − measure out your horse's feed at home so you feel confident when discussing the weights.

6

INTERNAL PARASITES

All horses have, to a lesser or greater degree, a burden of internal parasites. A programme of chemical control using anthelmintics must be adhered to from the age of four weeks and then on for the rest of the horse's life. Good pasture management, as previously discussed, will also help to control infestations.

WAYS IN WHICH PARASITES AFFECT A HORSE'S HEALTH

1) Primary damage to the gut linings which restrict the absorption of nutrients.

2) Secondary damage to the gut linings by stopping or reducing blood flow causing death of the tissue (necrosis). Food cannot pass normally through the dead portion which results in colic.

3) The larval stages of some worms travel through the walls of the intestine, enter the small arterioles then migrate through the arteries moving against the flow of blood. Some travel to the heart causing valve damage, inflammation and weakening. Such damage will never be corrected and may lead to death eventually.

109

4) The adult worms cause anaemia due to blood sucking. Ulceration, colic and diarrhoea may also occur.

THE PARASITE LIFE CYCLES

The strongyles

The most damaging and dangerous of all worms are the strongyles, of which there are two types: large and small. They are also known as redworms.

There are fifty species of large and small strongyles.

Large strongyles

The most serious is Strongylus vulgaris — reddish brown, 2–5 cm long. Others include Strongylus edentatus, Strongylus equinus and Triodontophorus species.

The larvae of these worms burrow into the intestinal wall then into the small arterioles of the blood supply. Migration along the arteries then occurs. Some larvae travel along the aorta causing damage to heart valves, others enter the renal artery which supplies the kidneys. Most remain in the anterior mesenteric artery which supplies the intestines. Here they cause arteritis and thrombosis (clot formation). Clots may break off and cause blockages in the arteries leading to the intestines and hind legs. The damaged arteries may be weakened and bulge — this is known as an anuerism which may collapse or burst without warning, causing death. Large strongyle larvae cause many cases of colic.

It takes between six and twelve months for the larvae to mature into egg-laying adults when they then return to the large intestine. The female worm attaches to the gut wall and sucks blood. She lays her eggs which are passed out in the dung onto the pasture.

The eggs hatch into Stage 1 larvae in as little as three days. After feeding they become Stage 2 larvae. The final stage is when they become infective Stage 3 larvae; this may be within seven days if conditions are favourable (warm and damp). These wait on the grass to be eaten by the horse. Once eaten, the larvae begin to migrate through the body and so the life cycle continues.

Signs of infestation include diarrhoea, loss of appetite, depression, colic, weight loss and hind leg lameness.

Small strongyles

There are around forty species of small strongyles, also known as small redworms. The life cycle takes between six and twelve weeks. The adult worms vary in size; they may be 4−26 mm in length. Small strongyles are less damaging than the large strongyles because the adults do not suck blood.

Eggs of the mature worm are passed out in the faeces. Within a week the infective larvae develop and are ingested by the horse. Larvae burrow into the gut lining where they remain until they reach maturity. They then emerge as egg-laying adults to continue the life cycle. The larvae may suck blood but most damage is caused by the effect of the burrowing into the intestine walls.

Signs of heavy infestation include diarrhoea or constipation, loss of appetite, colic and weight loss. The digestive functioning of the large intestine may be severely impaired. Foals are very susceptible, so brood mares must be treated regularly and kept on clean paddocks.

Roundworms (Ascarid. Parascaris equorum)

Also known as the white worm, this is a heavily-bodied worm up to 50 cm long which has a ten to twelve week life cycle. The adult worm lays the eggs in the small intestine and they are then passed out in the faeces. The eggs are very resistant to drying out.

The second stage larvae develop on the pasture within six weeks. Once ingested by the horse, the larvae hatch and penetrate the wall of the intestine and are carried by the circulatory system to the heart, liver and other organs. Eventually they migrate to the lungs, break through the blood vessels into the lungs and travel up the trachea to be eventually coughed up and swallowed. Once swallowed they mature in the small intestine into egg-laying adults.

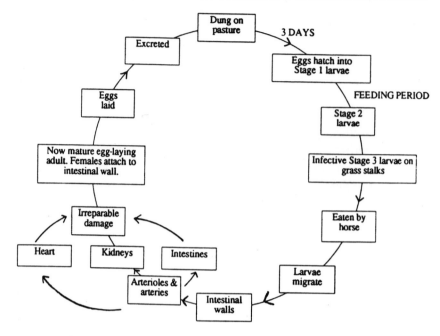

Figure 12 Life cycle of large strongyle, six to twelve months

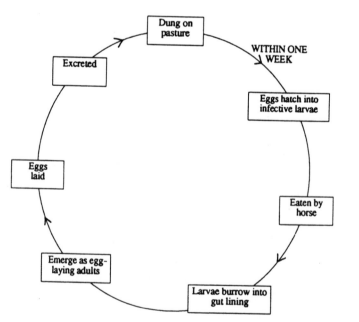

Figure 13 Life cycle of small strongyle, six to twelve weeks

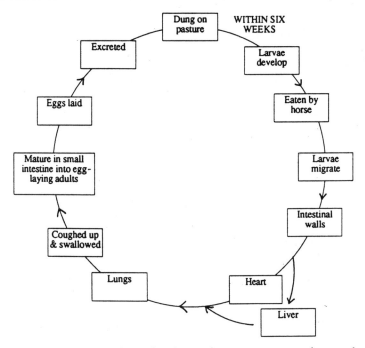

Figure 14 Life cycle of roundworm, ten to twelve weeks

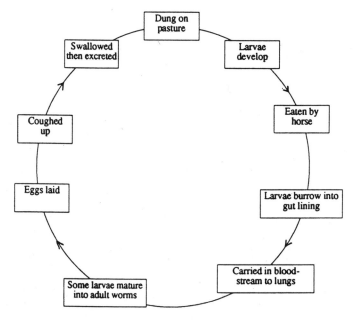

Figure 15 Life cycle of lungworm, approximately six weeks

Adult worms may cause obstructions and perforations of the intestines and bile duct. The risk to foals is great, causing haemorrhaging, coughing, severe enteritis and alternate diarrhoea and constipation. A heavy infestation will also cause a loss of condition and appetite followed by secondary infection.

Foals must be wormed first at four weeks old and from then on at four-weekly intervals. They should also only be turned out on clean pasture.

Lungworm (Dictyocaulus arnfieldi)

A long, slender worm, 25–60 mm in length.

The larvae are picked up by grazing horses and swallowed. The larvae then burrow through the intestinal walls and are carried in the blood to the lungs. The larvae which develop into adult worms do so in approximately six weeks, although many do not progress beyond the larval stage. If they do mature, eggs are laid, coughed up, swallowed and passed out in the droppings to await ingestion by another horse. The eggs only survive in warm, moist conditions.

Donkeys are the primary host for this parasite so must be tested and treated before being allowed to graze with horses.

The damage done by lungworm larvae includes irritation of the bronchi causing parasitic bronchitis. This results in coughing, wheezing, excessive production of mucus and loss of appetite. In very heavy infestations there may also be secondary respiratory infections, chronic pneumonia and a build-up of fluid in the lungs. Death may follow, particularly in foals. Any damage will be slow in repairing.

Pinworm (Oxyuris equi)

Pinworms are sometimes known as seatworms.

The male pinworm is approximately 1 cm long, while the female is much larger with a long, pin-like tail, the total length being approximately 15 cm.

Adult female worms migrate out of the anus and lay many sticky eggs around it. These become infective in approximately four days depending on the climate. The horse may rub or bite at the larvae which cause itching on his skin surface, thus causing them to drop into bedding, water or onto the pasture. The larvae may remain alive for up to twelve months.

The larvae may be ingested and will then penetrate the lining of the large intestine to mature. They then emerge into the gut as egg-laying adults. The time taken from ingestion of infective larvae to adult worm is approximately four to five months.

Heavy infestation will cause a loss of condition, intense itchiness around the anus and intestinal ulceration from the mucosal feeding of the larvae.

Stomach hairworm (Trichostrongylus axei)

The adult worm is tiny and hairlike, being approximately 0.5 cm in length.

Eggs are passed out in the faeces, developing into infective larvae within a week providing conditions are warm and moist.

These larvae are ingested and mature into adult worms in the glands of the stomach and in the small intestine. Here the hairworms irritate and erode the gut lining, damaging capillaries and lymph vessels, causing a loss of blood. This blood loss leads to anaemia, oedema (swollen tissue) and rapid loss of condition. The absorptive capacity of the intestine is greatly reduced, resulting in a dark diarrhoea.

As with most types of worms, foals are particularly at risk and all precautions must be taken to avoid infestation.

Large-mouthed stomach worm (Habronema species)

The adult worms are whitish, 10−25 cm long and lay their eggs whilst attached to the stomach wall. The eggs are passed out in the faeces where they develop into larvae. These larvae are then ingested by housefly or stablefly maggots which feed on the manure. The larvae develop within the maggots and are infective as the adult fly emerges from the pupae. The adult fly then deposits the larvae on the lips, nostrils and any open wound. The horse licks at the larvae, they are ingested and mature in the stomach.

Any Habronema larvae deposited onto open wounds will cause serious damage as they migrate and feed. Larvae deposited in the eyes cause photophobia (sensitivity to sunlight), watery eyes and wart-like lesions.

The adult worms within the stomach cause tumour-like growths which may rupture or block the passage of food from the stomach.

The large-mouthed stomach worm can be controlled by using fly sprays, strips and repellents in the field and stable to destroy or deter the secondary host, the stable- or house-fly.

Threadworm (Strongyloides westeri)

These are tiny hairlike worms, less than 1 cm long. The worms sometimes reproduce on the pasture but it is usual for the parasitic female worms to reproduce without the aid of the males.

The eggs are laid in the small intestine and pass out onto the pasture in the faeces. In warm damp weather the threadworm may mature and reproduce on the pasture, bypassing the parasitic stage. The larvae may be ingested normally by the horse or may enter the body by penetrating the skin. Foals will become infected through the mare's milk while feeding.

Larvae which have penetrated the skin enter the bloodstream and migrate to the lungs. From there, they travel up the trachea, are coughed up and swallowed. Once in the small intestine they mature into adult, egg-laying worms.

In a healthy horse the damage done to the intestinal lining will not cause ill-health. However, a very heavy burden will interfere with digestion which in foals causes acute diarrhoea, weakness and loss of condition.

The damage caused by larvae entering through the skin includes respiratory damage, dermatitis and skin irritations. These larvae may become dormant in the bloodstream and are inaccessible to treatment.

Neck threadworm (Onchocera species)

The microfilariae or larvae are 0.25 mm long and coiled. They are found in subcutaneous lymph spaces where they are picked up by the Culicoides midge. They remain in the mouth area of the midge for around four weeks and are transferred onto other hosts as the midge feeds.

They burrow into the ligamentous tissues of the neck which causes a restriction of neck movement. Another site for the maturation of adult worms is within the tendons of the legs, causing lameness.

Although this parasite does not affect the digestive system, it can be controlled with the use of certain anthelmintics. Insecticides and repellents must be used to control the Culicoides midge.

Tapeworm (Anoplocephala perfoliata)

The adult tapeworm is normally found in the caecum, often in large numbers at the ileocaecal junction. The mature adult measures 8−25 cm in length, 8−14 mm in width and attaches to the gut wall by four suckers.

Mature tapeworms shed segments which are passed in the dung; occasionally the whole worm is passed. The segments break down, releasing eggs onto the pasture. The eggs are eaten by the Oribatid mite, sometimes called forage mite, which acts as the secondary host. In the forage mite, the eggs develop into larval tapeworm known as cysticeroids. This takes approximately four months. The forage mite lives in the root mat, particularly on permanent pasture and may be ingested by the grazing horse. After a period of approximately eight weeks the cysticeroid breaks out and ruptures, releasing adult tapeworm segments which then mature in the horse's caecum.

Heavy infestations cause ulceration and blockages of the ileocaecal junction.

It is not always possible to determine the presence of tapeworms from a faecal examination as the techniques developed for showing roundworm infestations are not suitable.

In a recent study it was found that many horses have a

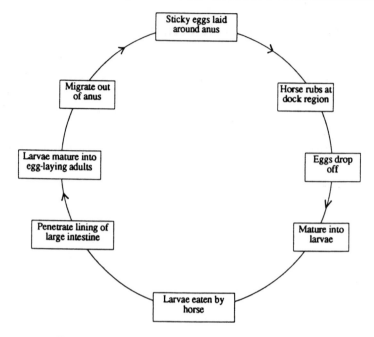

Figure 16 Life cycle of pinworm, four to five months

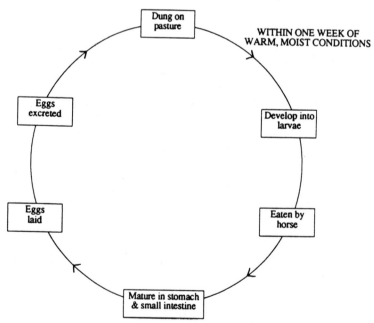

Figure 17 Life cycle of stomach hairworm

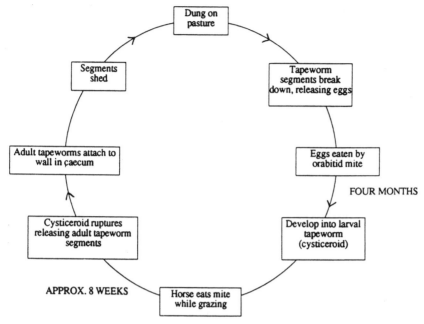

Figure 18 Life cycle of tapeworm, approximately six months

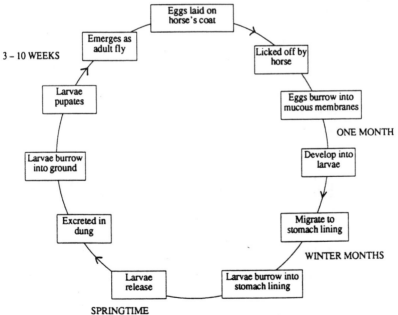

Figure 19 Life cycle of bot, ten to thirteen months

tapeworm burden which is unapparent. It is thought that they are a potential cause of ileocaecal intussuception. (The intestine turns in on itself: this can be compared to what can happen to the finger of a rubber glove, or to the closing of a telescope.) This is a recent phenomenon which may have arisen owing to modern wormers being so effective against roundworms that the field is left clear for tapeworms to gain a hold.

Bots (Gastrophilus species)

The adult botfly (Gastrophilus) is about 1.25 cm long and looks similar to a bee. The female fly is active in the early summer and September. The female fly lays the eggs in the horse's coat from where they are licked by the horse into his mouth. From here they burrow into the mucous membranes of the mouth, tongue and gums. In these warm, moist conditions the eggs develop into larvae and after a month, migrate to the stomach lining.

The mature larvae are reddish brown, approximately 2 cm long with a broad, rounded body tapering to a narrow hooked anterior. In the development period of eight to ten months, the larvae attach themselves to the stomach lining thus causing haemorrhaging, ulceration or perforation of the stomach. If not controlled this can lead to fatal peritonitis and intestinal block-age. These conditions may occur in the absence of symptoms.

In the spring the larvae release their hold and are passed out in the faeces, burrow into the ground and pupate. Within three to ten weeks the adult fly emerges and so the life cycle continues.

CONTROL OF WORM INFESTATION

This aspect of horse care may be divided into two categories:

1) Paddock management, as discussed fully earlier.

2) Chemical control using drugs (anthelmintics), fly repellents and insecticides.

A plan must be drawn up and records maintained.

Brood mares must be treated every six weeks, but note that some drugs are not suitable for pregnant mares. The pasture must also be clean. Once the foal is four weeks old he must be wormed and then treated every four weeks until he is eight months old. From eight months old he must be wormed every six to eight weeks for the rest of his life.

Horses out at grass must all be wormed at the same time. The stabled horse must be wormed every six to eight weeks because, during a spell at grass, he would have picked up redworm larvae which take approximately one year to become egg-laying adults. Therefore he may still have a worm burden and be suffering much damage due to migrating larvae.

Diagnosis of worm infestation

If desired, a quantitative check on the worm burden may be made using an egg count. Blood tests will show the level of damage caused by worms.

Egg counts: the worm eggs present in a sample of fresh faeces are counted under a microscope. This can be misleading, however, as there may be larvae migrating through the body that have been unaffected by any anthelmintics administered.

Blood tests: a particular type of white blood cell, eosinophil, will increase in numbers as an allergic reaction to the presence of migrating larvae. Globulins (blood proteins) increase when there is a worm infestation. These levels will show up in a blood test and are indicative of the levels of damage which may have occurred.

Blood tests may be of value when trying to determine the cause of loss of condition or performance.

Wormers

When deciding which brand of wormer to use, take into consideration their effectiveness against the adult stages of strongyles and ascarids as well as the suitability for use on stallions and pregnant mares.

The drugs available include:

Drug	Marketed as	Note
Thiabendazole	Equizole	Safe for pregnant mares.
Mebendazole	Telmin	
Pyrantel Embonate	Strongid-P	Double dosage needed to treat tapeworms. Safe for stallions and pregnant mares.
Dichlorvos	Equiguard	Effective against bots.
Ivermectin	Eqvalan	A very effective drug, active against all the parasites mentioned and migrating larvae — no other wormer can act against these at normal dosages.
Fenbendazole	Panacur	Kills eggs, adults and larval stages of large and small strongyles, if given at five times the normal dose over five days.

This is a basic list and does not cover all anthelmintics on the market.

Resistance to wormers

If one particular type of anthelmintic is used for long periods, certain species begin to demonstrate resistance and can quickly become dominant in the worm population as they are no longer controlled by the routine worming programme. No resistance has yet been seen to Strongid-P, however often used.

Resistance occurs against the benzimidazole group of wormers. This includes thiabendazole, mebendazole, fenbendazole, oxibendazole and oxfendazole. Worms which are resistant to one type will usually show 'cross-resistance'; that is resistance to other wormers from the same group. It is necessary, therefore, when alternating brands of wormer, to check on the active ingredient in order to minimize the risk of cross-resistance. The most resistant type of worm is the small strongyle (Trichonema species).

Pyrantel embonate (marketed as Strongid-P) kills worms in a different way from the benzimidazole groups and is unrelated to them in chemical structure. It is also effective against worms that have developed a resistance to this group of anthelmintics. It must be used in double dosages to kill tapeworms and it is recommended that this is done twice yearly with the exception of stallions and pregnant mares. It is effective against all round-worms, strongyles, pinworms and tapeworms but does not control bots.

Ivermectin (marketed as Eqvalan) is a very effective drug, killing all eggs, larvae and adult worms, even Strongylus vulgaris migrating through the arterial system. Ivermectin is also highly effective against bots and lungworm. Cross-resistance is unlikely to occur as Ivermectin is structurally unrelated to the benzimidazole or pyrantel compounds. It may be given safely to pregnant mares or to stallions. (Ivermectin has been shown to be poisonous to certain types of dogs. Care must be taken to avoid leaving used syringes around or allowing a dog to pick up food or paste droplets from the horse's mouth.)

Administering wormers

This may be done orally or by stomach tube.

Powders/Pellets can be mixed in with the normal feed. If you have a sensitive, fussy feeder, add a delicacy that you know he is fond of; molasses, fruit juice, beer or apples.

Pastes are fairly convenient to use providing you have a co-operative horse. Simply adjust the ring on the plunger shaft to give the correct dosage and squirt onto the back of the tongue. Try to keep the horse's head up and mouth closed; horses are often capable of spitting £8 worth of wormer onto the floor or down your arm.

If your horse is not happy about taking paste, disguise it amongst some minty tasting bread or titbits and either give by hand or mix in with the feed.

Administration by stomach tube. This has to be done by the vet and is usually only carried out when a very large dose of wormer needs to be administered.

7

INSTINCTIVE EQUINE BEHAVIOUR

All animals are born with innate reactions and inclinations known as instinct.

The ancestors of today's domesticated horse were wild creatures of the plains whose survival depended upon keen sensory systems to detect danger signals, and an effective defence mechanism to provide protection.

The dominating instincts of survival are present today in every horse or pony even though their survival is dependent upon the humans who look after them.

SURVIVAL

The horse's sensory systems provide the information needed to stimulate the instincts of survival.

Smell. The nostrils are able to detect edible feedstuffs, fresh water and airborne scents. Stallions can smell in-season mares. Horses use their sense of smell when 'getting to know' each other.

Hearing. The external ears are mobile enough to be able to catch distant sounds and direct them into the auditory canal. (The different movements of the ears also express the horse's different moods.)

Sight. The position of his eyes allows the horse a wide visual range even when grazing.

Feel. The whiskers act as feelers which help to prevent unwanted objects from being eaten. The skin is sensitive to touch so an unwanted presence can be dislodged.

Taste. This sense is closely associated with smell and helps the horse to avoid eating harmful and unpleasant plants. However, through desperation, starving horses may eat poisonous herbage.

The horse's sensory systems are discussed fully in another book in this series, *The Horse: Physiology.*

SUSTENANCE

In the wild, horses mainly used their sense of smell to seek fresh water and herbage, eating small amounts fairly constantly as they roamed. Their digestive system therefore developed in such a way that only small quantities could be contained in the stomach, while the intestines have the capacity to hold large amounts of roughage which may take several days to break down and be fully digested.

This fact must be taken into consideration when feeding the domesticated horse. It must also be remembered that horses have this instinct to roam and graze and should therefore have the opportunity to do so for at least a few hours a day. If it is not possible to turn the horse out, he should be grazed in hand — be understanding if he wants to wander about, picking at grass!

HERD MEMBERSHIP

Horses are naturally gregarious animals and instinctively feel 'safety in numbers', resulting in a very strong desire to stay within the herd. It is not ideal to keep a solitary horse — another horse, a pony, donkey or even a goat should be provided for companionship.

It can be stressful for a horse to be separated from the other members of his herd or group, as he may feel threatened; for example a horse left in his stable when all the others go out of the yard on exercise may become very upset. He may pace frantically around the stable, whinnying loudly and sweating up. In extreme cases he may try to jump out.

The ridden horse must, however, be trained to leave his 'herd' when asked. Youngsters will often 'nap' (refuse to go forwards, possibly rearing, whipping round suddenly or simply standing rooted to the spot). This has to be dealt with fairly and firmly. The trainer must instil in the horse confidence, respect and trust. The horse must be taught that it is safe to leave the herd; that dangerous behaviour will not be tolerated and that good behaviour will be rewarded. This does not, of course, happen overnight!

The stable often becomes the horse's 'safe house' — a substitute for the herd. This may explain why horses tend to walk out more freely and are less likely to nap on the way home from a hack, as they are keen to get home. A frightened horse instinctively returns to his stable or herd for safety. This may be seen when a horse breaks loose or when a rider has fallen off. The horse usually gallops back to the yard or, if at an event, to his lorry and tries to go to his companions; his fellow 'herd' members. In the event of a stable fire this instinct can have dangerous consequences. The horse becomes frightened because of the sounds, sights and smells of burning which compel him to remain in his safe house — his stable. In such cases it may be necessary to try and block the senses by covering the head with a damp jacket or towel. The horse may then allow himself to be led out of the stable.

THE DEFENCE SYSTEM

Once a horse has been alerted to danger the hormones adrenalin and noradrenalin are released in response. These prepare the body for flight or fight, hence they are known as the fright, flight, fight hormones.

Flight. The horse has evolved as a fast animal whose long legs allow him to gallop away from danger.

Fight. The horse can defend himself by the following means:

Kicking with the hind feet.
Striking out with the forefeet.
Biting.
Squashing a predator against a tree/scraping a predator off under a branch.
Bucking and rearing.

Horses are naturally wary of snakes and sudden, sharp movements. Most are frightened by a hosepipe being carelessly pulled around beneath them or of a trailing lead rope or lunge line as these provoke the instinctive fear of snakes.

COMMUNICATION

Horses use a wide range of signals to communicate how they feel both to fellow horses and their human handlers. The whole body is used but it is the facial expressions in particular which indicate how a horse is feeling.

A relaxed horse will appear bright-eyed with an inquisitive, interested expression, ears pricked forward. He will seem calm and generally at ease with his companions and surroundings.

A frightened horse may lay his ears back in an attempt to detect the sounds of danger, flare his nostrils to pick up smells and 'roll' his eyes to try and see the danger. This expression indicates that the 'fright, flight, fight' hormones have probably been released so the horse may resort to one or more of his defence mechanisms.

An angry or jealous horse may show the whites of his eyes, lay his ears flat back and bare his teeth, giving an aggressive, dominant expression. This can often be seen when a group of horses are fed in a field — there is a pecking order and the timid horses surrender their feed to the dominant ones: a factor which must be considered when feeding grass-kept horses.

Horses also use their 'body language' when being ridden. Tension and discomfort may be expressed through teeth grinding, tail clamping or swishing, arching of the back, unsteadiness in the mouth, bolting, rearing and napping. Horses may buck either through high spirits or in a malicious attempt to deposit the rider — it is usually fairly obvious which it is!

The rider must determine why a horse is showing signs of tension or behaving badly:

Is the horse in pain? For example from back or teeth problems or ill-fitting tack?

Does the horse lack confidence? Is he being asked to do more than he is able, both physically and mentally?

Is the handler consistently firm and fair? Does the handler have the expertise to train this horse?

Is the horse taking advantage of the trainer's lack of expertise and 'getting away with it'?

These are some of the questions to be asked under such circumstances. Having found the answers to these questions, steps can be taken to rectify the problem.

An excited horse will carry his tail high, prance about whether ridden or in the stable and his ears will prick to and fro. Eyes and nostrils will be wide open in order to take in all the sights and smells that are exciting him. Often horses will defecate or stale in their excitement. These signs are often seen in young horses out hunting for the first time or in a group of horses when the hunt goes past their yard or field.

By observing horses and their reactions to various stimuli, you can gain a greater understanding of what makes them 'tick'. An understanding of the instinctive reactions of the horse helps us to appreciate why horses behave in particular ways. This understanding should be used to build up a sympathetic and trusting rapport with every horse you handle and train.

STRESS

The word 'stress' can be applied to a broad spectrum of pressures or tension and can be described as a normal daily response to various stimuli placing demands on both physical and mental energies.

A certain amount of stress is desirable — without stress the body, both mental and physical, would never adapt and alter. Having responded to any given stimulus the body adapts in some way — the next time that stimulus is encountered it should be less stressful to the horse.

When stress is discussed in relation to the fittening and training of the competition horse, the main priority has to be that of introducing new levels of stress carefully under a monitored training programme. In this way stress is used positively to the benefit of the horse.

In training, almost every part of the body is under some degree of stress. It is knowing the acceptable degree of stress which prevents actual harm being caused. If this degree is exceeded for any length of time the horse becomes distressed as he cannot cope with constant stress. Distress is a situation that should be avoided whenever possible.

Physical causes of stress can include:

1) Birth. A natural stress to both dam and offspring, evoking strong instincts of protection and survival.

2) Pain. Due to injury, disease, castration of the young colt, cruel treatment etc.

3) Illness. The immune system is depressed when the horse is under stress — good nursing is essential.

4) Hunger and thirst. Thirst is particularly distressing to any animal.

5) Competing. Whether performing a dressage test or jumping and galloping, competition places stress on the horse.

6) Long journeys. These become more stressful if the ventilation is inadequate, conditions cramped and no provision made for refreshment.

7) Crowds of horses/people. The excitement and general activity associated with large crowds causes stress.

8) Exhaustion and fatigue. All the horse's systems are over-stressed when he is exhausted, this leads to distress.

9) Conflict. The wild horse adapts to cope with the stress of physical conflict.

Mental causes of stress can include:

1) Environment. An unstable, disorganized environment with a 'bad' atmosphere is stressful, for example a sale ring or badly run yard.

2) Change of environment. A horse who has been used to a happy atmosphere in a well run yard will feel stressed when moved, particularly if moved to an environment as described above.

3) Weaning. With careful planning, weaning may be done with minimum upset. By its very nature it is still, however, stressful to both dam and offspring.

4) Breaking. When it is done slowly and patiently, stress can be reduced in the early days of training.

5) Confusion and uncertainty, such as inconsistency from the handler/trainer or frequent changes of environment.

6) Boredom and loneliness. As horses are gregarious they do not enjoy living alone and are very stressed by boredom.

7) Fear. Fear can be caused by many things such as being overfaced when jumping or bad treatment in the yard. Also, horses sense when a human is afraid, this leads to a loss of respect and/or confidence in that person.

Depending upon the nature of the stimulus, the horse's reaction to stress may be physiological or psychological. Disturbance of the horse's psychological balance may lead to behavioural problems.

Physiological reactions may include:

1) Sweating.

2) Shivering.

3) Release of adrenalin.

4) Increase or decrease in temperature, pulse and respiratory rates.

5) Strain or tear to muscles and tendons.

6) Exostosis or fracture of bone.

7) Onset of disease.

8) Excessive defecating and/or urinating.

Psychological reactions may show as a combination of the following behavioural problems:

1) Box-walking.

2) Windsucking.

3) Crib-biting.

4) Bolting.

5) Rearing.

6) Biting and kicking.

7) Weaving.

8) Refusing to jump.

9) Refusing to be caught or handled.

These psychological reactions may be highly negative. The horse in his wild state copes with physical stress with instinctive reactions. When our stabled, domesticated horses have no such way of dealing with the mental stress inflicted upon them, the result is often the development of one or more of the so-called 'vices'.

STABLE VICES: AVOIDANCE

The majority of vices developed by stabled horses are a direct result of boredom due to long periods of confinement in the loose box. It should be borne in mind that the horse is naturally 'a wanderer', enjoying out-of-doors freedom.

To counteract boredom and reduce mental stress:

1) Turn the horse out daily for long periods.

2) If turning out is not possible, lead out and graze in hand.

3) Divide the exercise into two lots: this is often only possible in a yard with sufficient staff.

4) Divide feeds up, so adhering to the rule 'little and often'. Eating alleviates boredom.

5) Ensure a constant supply of good quality hay.

6) Stable the horse in a position to see all yard activities.

7) Provide some sort of 'toy', for example a mangel, sugarbeet or suchlike with string through the middle, tied in such a position that the horse can play with it. There is now a specially manufactured 'horse toy' called the 'Pasafier', a durable rotating device which can be positioned in the stable. The horse is attracted to the apple flavouring on the centre wheel and although he is unable to grasp the wheel he can play with the Pasafier for hours.

8) Provide a salt/mineral lick in the stable.

TYPES OF VICE: CONTROL AND REMEDY

Crib-biting and windsucking

Crib-biters take hold of any projecting object such as the stable door or paddock railings and gulp in air. Windsuckers arch their neck and gulp in air, usually without taking hold of anything.

These vices are serious and constitute unsoundness. The habits cannot be broken, but can be controlled. The teeth wear down more quickly on a crib-biter, therefore the tables of the teeth give the appearance of an older mouth.

Taking air into the stomach may cause colic and some loss of condition.

Control crib-biting by painting all exposed woodwork with an anti-chew mixture such as creosote. Ideally the stable should be lined with kickboards extending above head height. This reduces the chance of the horse crib-biting on any ledges. The top of the lower half of the stable door must have a protective metal strip. The main disadvantage of smearing anything such as 'Cribox' on the lower door is that tack, rugs, horse and handler tend to get covered in the sticky paste as well.

An anti-crib strap prevents the horse from gulping in air. It must be fitted securely but obviously not too tightly. It is not safe to turn a horse out in one.

There are many sorts of muzzle available, all of which allow the horse to drink. Some allow the horse to eat as well, although if crib-biting is to be controlled the mouth does have to be covered. A metal grille may be used on the top half of the door so the horse may still see out, but cannot bite the stable door.

Employ all of the ideas discussed to help alleviate boredom. Remember also that other horses in the yard may try to copy the crib-biting horse.

Weaving

A weaving horse stands rocking or swaying from side to side, swinging his head as he does so. This is a serious vice and constitutes an unsoundness. The problem is normally caused through boredom and/or nervous tension. Again, alleviate boredom wherever possible.

An anti-weaving grid may help, although the confirmed, neurotic weaver will stand behind the grid and weave.

It has been suggested that hanging objects such as water-filled plastic bottles over the door may help. Unfortunately for the owner, it is very much trial and error to find a method of control for this vice.

Since constant weaving puts a strain on the legs, ensure the horse has a well-bedded stable.

Box-walking

Because of boredom and/or nervous tension the horse paces around in circles in the stable, churning up the bedding and often sweating. If nervous tension appears to be the main cause, the origin should be sought and the work and feed regime investigated.

The main solution is to prevent boredom, in particular by turning out as much as possible and by providing companionship in the form of a pony, sheep or goat.

Tearing clothing

The horse chews at rugs and bandages, ripping them in the process. This may be due to an area of irritation beneath the clothing, or boredom. Occasionally very young horses may tear their rugs when worn for the first few occasions.

To remedy:

1) Check for any skin complaint which may cause the irritation.

2) Dab bitter aloes on the clothing.

3) Alleviate boredom.

4) Use a bib fastened to the underneath of a leather headcollar.

5) Use a muzzle.

Eating droppings

This may be caused through boredom or a craving for minerals.
   To remedy:

1) Alleviate boredom.

2) Keep stable very clean.

3) Provide a mineral lick.

4) Add mineral supplement to feeds.

Biting and snapping

This vice can vary from the harmless character who stands pulling faces at you to the rather more disconcerting one who lunges at you from the back of the stable, teeth bared. The cause is often mismanagement, particularly in the early stages of handling when the youngster nips playfully.

Some horses are sensitive or thin-skinned and dislike being groomed or rugged up roughly or carelessly. The feeding of titbits can also lead to biting.

To remedy:

1) Treat the horse fairly and firmly, reprimanding him quickly if he actually bites you. A quick slap on the side of the muzzle is normally enough punishment.

2) Grooming and rugging up must always be carefully carried out. When tightening girths and rollers, take care not to pinch the horse.

3) If used, only feed titbits after a period of work, when the horse deserves his reward.

4) Confirmed biters must be tied up when being groomed or rugged up and should wear a muzzle at other times.

Kicking at walls

Horses will kick at the stable walls or door for a number of reasons:

1) Irritability. A horse may want his food or to be turned out with the other horses.

2) Rats and mice. Many horses become upset if they know rats are running about in their bedding.

3) Parasites and skin irritation. A horse with lice or grease may kick at the wall or water bucket as a means of scratching a leg.

4) Boredom. He may simply like the noise.

To remedy:

1) Pad or line the walls to deaden the sound.

2) If necessary, put down poison for vermin. This must, of course, be done in such a way as to avoid ingestion by horses, dogs, chickens etc.

3) Alleviate boredom.

4) If extreme, put hobbles on the hind legs.

Kicking at handler

This is a most disconcerting vice, because of the damage that a shod foot can do.

The causes are very much the same as for biting and must be dealt with firmly and effectively. When grooming a kicker try to stay as close to his body as possible to minimize the chance of his shod foot striking you. When grooming the hind legs, get someone to hold up a front foot and grasp his tail firmly, holding it to one side; this often works with kickers.

If the kicking is due to sensitive skin, try to be more considerate when grooming and only use a very soft body brush. Some horses are abnormally sensitive and just cannot stand harsh brushing. Such horses must be handled considerately, otherwise their behaviour will degenerate and an avoidable accident may result.

Remember when exercising a kicker in company to tie a red ribbon at the top of the tail to warn other riders.

HANDLING THE FRACTIOUS HORSE

There are occasions when horses are not co-operative when being handled. This is particularly evident when horses are difficult to clip, shoe or when having their teeth rasped.

Some of the most common causes of bad behaviour are:

1) Fear. The memory of a previous bad experience.

2) Lack of training. The young horse should be taught to stand whilst being handled. Picking out feet and introduction to clippers should be included in early training.

3) Bad handling. The skill of the handler makes a great difference in some instances.

4) Nervousness. Some horses are genuinely nervous even though they have had no previous bad experiences.

5) Sheer bad temper. Having taken into account the above, there are still some horses who are plain 'bolshy' and bad-tempered.

Methods of restraint

Bridle. It is impossible to control a fractious horse properly in a headcollar, so a bridle is needed.

Hobbles. The hind legs are tied to each other using a specially designed arrangement of leather straps. The horse may kick violently in an attempt to remove them, so they are not ideal.

Holding or strapping up a foreleg. This may work but the majority of horses are perfectly capable of throwing themselves around on three legs. If a strap is used it must be of a 'quick release' design.

Twitching. The old-fashioned twitch consists of a loop of strong, thick string attached to the top of a wooden pole. Modern twitches are metal with a 'nutcracker' type action and are easier to use than the old-fashioned type.

The twitch is applied to the gristly upper lip and held quite tightly. With the old type, the string loop is passed over the lip and the wooden pole turned to tighten the loop. The metal twitch is simply closed over the upper lip and held.

Originally the twitch was thought to distract the horse by causing severe discomfort, so making him more biddable. Current research has shown this is probably not the reason why the twitch is so effective. It is now thought that the twitch acts in a manner similar to acupuncture, in that its pressure causes endorphins to be released into the bloodstream. Endorphins are morphine-like, natural analgesics produced within the body which actually reduce the horse's awareness of pain and aid relaxation.

A twitch must *never* be used anywhere other than on the upper lip. Once released, the lip should be hand massaged to promote circulation.

Firm pressure applied to the horse's nasal passages by hand is sometimes sufficient, as is taking a good pinch of skin on the horse's neck and holding securely.

Whenever dealing with a difficult horse, do not start in an aggressive or defensive frame of mind. Speak to the horse quietly and try to gain his trust before resorting to your method of restraint.

Never position yourself in such a way that you are at risk of being jumped on; stand to the side of him. If you have an assistant, ensure you both stand on the same side to lessen the risks of injury.

Whenever handling an awkward horse take extra safety precautions such as wearing a crash cap and gloves. Remove any extra objects, such as haynets and buckets, from the stable to reduce the risk of injury.

SEDATION

Sedation may be employed for the following reasons:

1) To calm a fractious horse to facilitate procedures such as clipping and teeth rasping.

2) In combination with a local anaesthetic to allow stitching of injuries.

3) As a premedication in preparation for general anaesthesia.

It is not generally considered safe to sedate a horse prior to travelling as he needs to be alert enough to balance himself during the journey.

There is a wide range of sedating and tranquillizing agents, the administration of which should be under the guidance of the vet. Some horses react badly to sedatives, becoming seriously unsettled as the drug wears off. There are other side-effects to be considered also.

Sedatives are substances which produce mild depression of the central nervous system, making the horse calm, possibly drowsy.

Tranquillizers reduce anxiety without producing excessive drowsiness or otherwise impairing consciousness.

Opiates are substances derived from opium and have a narcotic (sleep inducing) effect although they do not produce marked sedation on their own.

Sedatives, tranquillizers and opiates are used in combination to produce profound sedation whilst still allowing the horse to stand. The combinations used will very much depend upon the vet's personal preference.

Sedatives

Xylazine. This drug is very useful for premedication as well as standing sedation. It may be given intravenously which produces a faster-acting effect and is more cost-effective. If given intramuscularly, three times the dosage is needed. The effect lasts for approximately half an hour and recovery is fast and complete.

Detomidine. A relatively new drug similar to Xylazine.

Tranquillizers

Acepromazine (ACP) is a very popular and widely used tranquillizer which does not sedate deeply. Acepromazine may be given intravenously, whereby it takes effect in about fifteen minutes, or intramuscularly, in which case it can take an hour before the horse begins to appear tranquil. The drug may also be administered orally in tablet form.

A very popular and effective combination is that of Xylazine and Acepromazine which produces a deeper state of sedation.

Opiates

These are normally used in combination with other drugs.

Etorphine is a very potent derivative of morphine which is not used on its own.

Immobilon is the name of a drug produced as a result of combining Acepromazine and Etorphine. It is often used for short surgical procedures. This drug acts in around two minutes and the horse falls to the ground. There are some important side-effects to consider when Immobilon is used. These include depression of the respiratory system, cyanosis (blueing) of the mucous membranes, increase in pulse rate to around 120 beats per minute and a dramatic rise in the arterial blood pressure.

Revivon. After the use of Immobilon, Revivon is injected intravenously to bring the horse round again. Within approximately ninety seconds the horse comes round and gets to his feet. Once standing, the horse may try to wander around aimlessly so it is essential that an assistant walks with him to prevent injury. This walking may last for several hours.

Approximately four hours after the initial injection the horse may show the effects of Etorphine once again. This is due to the reabsorption of the Etorphine from the bile. If these effects are shown again the vet will administer a further dose of Revivon.

The use of sedatives, tranquillizers and similar drugs must be very carefully monitored by the vet. There are other drugs in regular use, dependent upon individual vets' preferences.

A good knowledge of the physiological side-effects of each drug is essential in order to avoid causing serious harm. It must, of course, be remembered that all horses are individuals and can be affected in different ways by different drugs.

THE CAST HORSE

This is one of the situations that all horse owners dread finding their horse in — cast, unable to get up having laid down to roll in the stable.

Preventative measures

These measures can help prevent a horse from becoming cast:

1) Ensure that the stable is roomy enough for the horse. He will be less likely to get wedged up against a wall when rolling if he is in a large stable.

2) If planning new stables, curve the flooring material up the lower 30 cm (12 in) of the wall.

3) Ensure that bedding is always level, with well-banked sides. Bedding must always be of a good depth and kept as even as possible. Some horses dig up their shavings before rolling and then become cast because of the hole.

4) Use an anti-cast roller at all times. Horses who are specially prone to getting cast should wear the roller even when not wearing a rug. A breast strap will prevent the roller (which should be well padded) from slipping backwards. Although anti-cast rollers prevent the horse from rolling completely over, unfortunately, in some circumstances, the horse may still become cast.

5) Block in any spaces below fixed mangers because a horse can get his legs beneath the manger once he has lain down.

6) Never leave manger or bucket holders empty.

7) Remove empty haynets and always be sure they are not low enough to catch a rolling horse's leg.

Dealing with the cast horse

1) Remain calm.

2) If the horse is lying calmly on his back it may be possible to pass a lunge line behind his outside hind and fore legs. An assistant should ideally be at the head, and the head turned as the legs are pulled over.

3) Always be wary of the hooves, particularly as the horse gets to his feet.

4) If the horse is thrashing about do not enter the stable because the risk of being badly hurt is too great. Try to calm the horse by using your voice in a soothing manner. If you suspect that the horse has hurt himself in any way, call the vet quickly.

5) Very often the horse will thrash about for a minute or so then lie still to catch his breath before thrashing about again. Although it is nerve-racking to watch, the horse usually manages to kick himself out of trouble, although he may have some cuts and bruises as a result.

If he still fails to rise, enter the stable only with a knowledge-able assistant or the vet and attempt to pass the lines behind his legs. It may be necessary for the vet to sedate the horse if it is not possible to pass the lunge line behind his hind legs. Always be sure that you do not place yourself in a vulnerable position.

Placing extra bedding, such as sections of a straw bale, in strategic positions can help the horse to rise and may also soften some of the blows as the horse kicks at the wall.

The method of dealing with a cast horse will always be influenced by the horse's temperament and the handler's experience; if in any doubt the horse is best left to sort himself out whilst under close observation. Expert help should, however, be sought if he still fails to rise, as he may injure himself. His circulatory system will not function normally if he is down for a prolonged period.

CONCLUSION

Good management of the horse results from understanding and attending to both his physical and mental requirements.

The physical requirements can be summarized thus:

1) Provide the best form of housing for the horse, in a safe and well organized yard.

2) Provide a clean, deep and dust-free bed together with a constant supply of fresh water.

3) Adhere to the main rules of feeding.

4) Ensure that the horse is exercised regularly and whenever possible turned out to grass for mental and physical relaxation.

5) Keep the horse clean with regular grooming, providing warmth with rugs and blankets.

6) Attend to his health needs: regular visits to the farrier, regular worming, teeth rasping and inoculations. Call the vet whenever necessary.

Through the provision of a safe and healthy environment, you are halfway to having a happy and healthy horse. However, even in the most luxurious stable a horse will not be happy if he is caused mental stress. Therefore:

1) Try to understand the horse's instincts and natural desires.

Bearing these in mind it is important to provide companion-ship; loneliness is stressful to a herd animal.

2) Treat the horse fairly, firmly and with consideration. Horses always remember rough handling and soon lose their trust.

3) Always talk to your horse. He may not understand what you say, but will enjoy hearing your voice.

4) Reduce boredom to a minimum.

5) Keep as close as possible to a routine, horses feel secure when they know 'what happens next'.

Taking the time and trouble to observe the horse, understand his behaviour, and provide for his physical and mental needs, will ensure that you have provided the highest quality of care, resulting in a healthy and contented horse.

BIBLIOGRAPHY

Houghton-Brown, J. and Powell-Smith, V. *Horse and Stable Management*. Collins, 1985.

Pilliner, S. *Getting Horses Fit*. Collins, 1986.

Roberts, M.B.V. *Biology — A Functional Approach*. Thomas Nelson and Son Ltd., 1979.

Snow, Dr. D.H. and Vogel, C.J. *Equine Fitness — The Care and Training of the Athletic Horse*. David and Charles, 1987.

McCarthy, Gillian. *Pasture Management for Horses & Ponies*. B.S.P. Professional Books, 1988.

INDEX